A Short Introduction to the Tiberian Masoretic Bible and its Reading Tradition

Gorgias Handbooks

Series Editor

George Anton Kiraz

Gorgias Handbooks provides students and scholars with reference books, textbooks and introductions to different topics or fields of study. In this series, Gorgias welcomes books that are able to communicate information, ideas and concepts effectively and concisely, with useful reference bibliographies for further study.

A Short Introduction to the Tiberian Masoretic Bible and its Reading Tradition

Second Edition

Geoffrey Khan

gorgias press

2013

Gorgias Press LLC, 954 River Road, Piscataway, NJ, 08854, USA

www.gorgiaspress.com

2013   ,

ISBN 978-1-4632-0246-0   ISSN 1935-6838

**Library of Congress Cataloging-in-Publication
Data**

Khan, Geoffrey.
   A short introduction to the Tiberian
Masoretic Bible and its reading tradition / by
Geoffrey Khan. -- Second edition.
        pages cm. -- (Gorgias handbooks)
   Includes bibliographical references and
indexes.
   ISBN 978-1-4632-0246-0
 1. Masorah. 2. Bible. Old
Testament--Criticism, Textual. 3. Bible. Old
Testament--Accents and accentuation. 4. Hebrew
language--Accents and accentuation. 5.
Cantillation. I. Title.
   BS718.K48 2013
   221.4'46--dc23

2013042537

Printed in the United States of America

TABLE OF CONTENTS

PREFACE

This small book is intended to provide a short introductory overview of the Tiberian Masoretic tradition of the Hebrew Bible and its background. It was this tradition that produced the great Masoretic codices of the Middle Ages, which form the basis of modern printed editions of the Hebrew Bible. The presentation gives particular prominence to the multi-layered nature of the Masoretic tradition. These layers include the various components of the written text surviving in the medieval Masoretic manuscripts as well as the reading tradition that was transmitted orally in the Middle Ages. Particular attention is given to the Tiberian reading tradition. Much of our current knowledge of this reading tradition, which is essential for a correct understanding of the Tiberian vocalization system, derives from recently discovered medieval sources and has not been incorporated so far into the standard textbooks of Biblical Hebrew used by students.

I acknowledge with gratitude the permission granted to me by the Ben-Zvi Institute in Jerusalem to reproduce plates of the Aleppo codex. I should also like to thank Nadia Vidro for carefully proof-reading the book and offering several valuable comments.

This second edition contains a number of additions to the first edition, notably in the chapters on Masoretic Treatises and on the Tiberian Pronunciation Tradition.

Geoffrey Khan
Cambridge

1. THE TIBERIAN MASORETIC TRADITION

The printed editions of the Hebrew Bible that are in use today are based on medieval manuscripts deriving from the school of the Masoretes of Tiberias. The Masoretes (known in Hebrew as בַּעֲלֵי מָסֹרָה) were scholars who devoted themselves to preserving the traditions of writing and reading the Bible. Their name derives from the Hebrew term *masorah* or *masoret*, the meaning of which is generally thought to be 'transmission of traditions'.[1] The Tiberian Masoretes were active over a period of several centuries in the second half of the first millennium C.E. The medieval sources refer to several generations of Masoretes, some of them belonging to the same family. The most famous of these families is that of Aharon ben Asher (tenth century), whose forebears were engaged in Masoretic activities over five generations.[2] The Masoretes continued the work of the *sopherim* ('scribes') of the Talmudic and

---

[1] There is no complete consensus concerning the original meaning or etymology of the term. It seems to be connected with the Rabbinic Hebrew verb מָסַר 'to hand over', though this may be a denominal form. The noun מְסֹרֶת occurs in Ezek. 20.37, which is generally understood today as 'bond' (< אסר). One of its ancient interpretations, however, was 'number' (cf. Septuagint ἀριθμῷ). As we shall see, counting letters and words to ensure the correct preservation of the text was one of the activities of the Masoretes. The word occurs also in Mishnah *Avot* 3.14 in a statement attributed to Rabbi Aqiva (c. 50–135 C.E.) מסרת סיג לתורה 'The *masoret* is a fence for the Torah', where it may have been originally used with the same sense (i.e. 'counting' of letters/words). Ben-Ḥayyim (1957) has suggested that the verb מסר in Hebrew actually had the meaning of 'to count', as did its cognate in Samaritan Aramaic. The form מְסֹרָה is a variant feminine pattern of the noun. The form מַסֹּרֶת or מָסֹרָה, which is reflected in the English spelling 'Massorah', has no textual basis but is a modern reconstruction on the analogy of the pattern found in nouns such as כַּפֹּרֶת 'mercy seat' and בַּצֹּרֶת 'dearth'.

[2] Asher 'the elder', the great-great-grandfather of Aharon, probably lived in the second half of the eighth century C.E.; cf. Kahle (1959, 75–82; 1927, vol. 1, 39).

Second Temple periods, who were also occupied with the correct transmission of the biblical text.[3]

The Tiberian Masoretes developed what can be termed the Tiberian Masoretic tradition. This was a body of tradition that gradually took shape over two or three centuries and continued to grow until it was finally fixed and the activities of the Masoretes ceased at the beginning of the second millennium. During the same period, circles of Masoretes are known to have existed also in Iraq. It is the tradition of the Tiberian Masoretes, however, that had become virtually the exclusive Masoretic tradition in Judaism by the late Middle Ages and has been followed by all printed editions of the Hebrew Bible.

The Tiberian Masoretic tradition is recorded in numerous medieval manuscripts. The majority of these were written after 1100 C.E. and are copies of older manuscripts that were made in various Jewish communities. The earlier printed editions are based on these late medieval manuscripts. The most authoritative of these early editions was the so-called second Rabbinic Bible (i.e. the Bible text combined with commentaries and translations, known as *Miqraʾot Gedolot*) edited by Jacob ben Ḥayyim ben Adoniyahu and printed at the press of Daniel Bomberg in Venice between 1524 and 1525. These early Rabbinic Bibles appear to have been based on more than one manuscript (Penkower 1983). This came to be regarded as a textus receptus and was used as the basis for many subsequent editions of the Hebrew Bible.

A small number of surviving manuscripts are first-hand records of the Tiberian Masoretic tradition. These were written in the Near East before

---

[3] According to the Babylonian Talmud (*Qiddushin* 30a) the *sopherim* acquired their name from the fact that they counted (Hebrew ספר) all the letters of the Pentateuch. As we have seen above (n.1) the term מָסֹרֶת was probably originally understood in the sense of 'counting'. This connection with the Talmudic interpretation of the term *sopherim* may be more than coincidental, in that מָסֹרֶת may have been intended originally to refer to the activity of the *sopherim*. In the Middle Ages the term *sopher* acquired the narrower sense of 'copyist'. According to a medieval list of Masoretes published by Mann (1972, vol. 2, 44) the chain of Masoretes began with Ezra the scribe.

1100 C.E., when the Masoretes were still active. They are, therefore, the most reliable witnesses of the Tiberian Masoretic tradition. They all come from the end, or near the end, of the Masoretic period, when the Masoretic tradition had become fixed in most of its details. The earliest dated manuscript in this corpus was written in the ninth century. After 1100 C.E. the fixed tradition was transmitted by generations of scribes. Some of the modern editions of the Bible are based on these early manuscripts, e.g. the *Biblia Hebraica* from the third edition (1929–1937) onwards (the latest edition of which is the *Biblia Hebraica Quinta*, 2004–), *The Hebrew University Bible* (1975–), the editions by A. Dotan (1973; revised 2001) and M. Breuer (1977–1982) and the modern edition of the Rabbinic Bible by M. Cohen (known as *Ha-Keter*, Ramat-Gan, 1992—).

The Tiberian Masoretic tradition can be divided into the following components:

1. The consonantal text of the Hebrew Bible.

2. The layout of the text and codicological form of the manuscripts.

3. The indications of divisions of paragraphs (known in Hebrew as *pisqaʾot* or *parashiyyot*).

4. The accent signs, which indicated the musical cantillation of the text and also the position of the main stress in a word.

5. The vocalization, which indicated the pronunciation of the vowels and some details of the pronunciation of the consonants in the reading of the text.

6. Notes on the text, written in the margins of the manuscript.

7. Masoretic treatises. Some manuscripts have appendices at the end of the biblical text containing various treatises on aspects of the teachings of the Masoretes.

8. Orally transmitted reading tradition.

The first seven of these components are written, whereas the eighth existed only orally. The orally transmitted reading tradition was passed on from one generation to the next during the Masoretic period. This reading tradition is partially represented in graphic form by the accent signs and the vocalization signs and is described to a certain extent in the Masoretic treatises. These written components of the Masoretic tradition, however, do not record all details of the reading tradition, especially with regard to the pronunciation of the consonants. The orally transmitted Tiberian reading tradition, therefore, should be treated as an additional component of the Tiberian Masoretic tradition. This reading tradition complemented the consonantal text, but it was independent of it to a certain degree, as is shown by the fact that the vocalization signs sometimes reflect a different reading from what is represented by the consonantal text. In such cases the traditional Masoretic terminology distinguishes between the *qere* ('what is read') from the *ketiv* ('what is written').

It is this complex of components, written and oral, that formed the Tiberian Masoretic tradition. A careful distinction must be made between the components of this tradition that the Masoretes had a direct role in creating and the components that were inherited from an earlier period. The core components that were inherited from earlier tradition include the consonantal text, the paragraph divisions, the oral reading tradition and some of the contents of the textual notes. The other components, i.e. the accent and vocalization signs (but not the reading tradition that the signs represented) and the majority of the textual notes and treatises, were developed by the Masoretes in the Masoretic period.

At the end of the Masoretic period the written components of the Tiberian Masoretic tradition had become fixed and were transmitted in this fixed form by later scribes. By contrast, the oral component, i.e. the Tiberian reading tradition, was soon forgotten and appears not to have been transmitted much beyond the twelfth century.

The Tiberian Masoretes did not develop a completely uniform tradition. Within the Tiberian school there were various streams of tradition that differed from one another in small details. These different streams were associated with the names of individual Masoretes. The differences that we know the most about were between Aharon ben Asher and Moshe ben Naphtali, who belonged to the last generation of Masoretes in the tenth century. The points of disagreement between these two Masoretes are recorded in lists at the end of many of the early Tiberian Bible manuscripts. They were collected by Misha'el ben 'Uzzi'el in an Arabic treatise known as *Kitāb al-Khilaf* 'The Book of Differences' (ed. Lipshütz 1965). These differences are only in very minor details. Roughly three quarters concern the placement of the so-called *ga'ya* sign (later known as the *meteg*), which supplements the accent signs mainly for the purpose of marking secondary stress in words. There is agreement on the consonantal text, and also, in virtually all cases, on the vocalization and accent signs. The existence of these lists of differences reflects the process of fixing and standardizing of the Masoretic tradition. We know from other sources about a number of differences between Masoretes of the preceding generations in the ninth century.[4] Again these concern only minor details. At the closure of the Masoretic period, after the generation of Aharon ben Asher, the Tiberian Masoretic tradition had not fixed on the school of one particular Masorete. A source from the eleventh century refers to the possibility of following either the school of Ben Asher or that of Ben Naphtali, without any evaluation (Eldar 1980a).

The Ben Asher school finally became supreme only when it was espoused by the influential Jewish scholar Moses Maimonides (1135-1204). When he was resident in Egypt, Maimonides examined a manuscript with vocalization and accents written by the hand of Aharon ben Asher and pronounced it to be the model that should be followed. It is likely that the book of differences between Ben Asher and Ben Naphtali (*Kitāb al-Khilaf*) was composed by Misha'el ben 'Uzzi'el shortly after this pronouncement of Maimonides.

The Tiberian Masoretic manuscripts are codices, i.e. books consisting of collections of double-leaves that were stitched together (known in Hebrew sources as *miṣhaph* < Arabic *muṣhaf*). The Hebrew Bible began to be produced in codex form during the Islamic period. The earliest surviving codices with explicitly dated colophons were written in the tenth century C.E. All of these originate from the Jewish communities in the Middle East (Beit-Arié et al. 1997). There is indirect evidence from some Rabbinic sources that

---

[4] Cf. the texts published in Yeivin (1981).

the codex had been adopted for Hebrew Bibles already in the eighth century
C.E. (Glatzer 1989, 260–261).

Previously, the Hebrew Bible was always written in a scroll. After the
introduction of the codex, scrolls continued to be used for writing the Hebrew Bible. Each type of manuscript, however, had a different function. The
scrolls were used for public liturgical reading in the synagogues whereas the
codices were used for study purposes and non-liturgical reading. The scroll
was the ancient form of manuscript that was hallowed by liturgical tradition
and it was regarded as unacceptable by the Masoretes to change the custom
of writing the scroll by adding the various written components of the
Masoretic tradition that they developed, such as vocalization, accents and
marginal notes. The codex had no such tradition behind it in Judaism and so
the Masoretes felt free to introduce into these types of manuscript the newly
developed written Masoretic components.[5] The desire to commit to writing
in the Middle Ages many components of the Masoretic tradition that had
been previously transmitted orally was no doubt one of the main motiva-
tions for the adoption of the codex at this period. It had been available as a
format of book production since the Roman period. It started to be used for
the writing of Christian Bibles as early as the second century C.E. The earliest extant datable codices of the Qurʾān pre-date the dated codices of the
Hebrew Bible by about two centuries. The fact that the medieval Hebrew
term for Bible, miṣḥaph, is a loanword from Arabic (muṣḥaf) suggests, indeed, that the Jews borrowed the format from the Muslims. We may say
that the liturgical scroll remained the core of the biblical tradition whereas
the Masoretic codex was conceived as auxiliary to this. This distinction of
function between liturgical scrolls with no vocalization, accents or Masoretic
notes, on the one hand, and Masoretic codices on the other has continued in
Jewish communities down to the present day. Occasionally in the Middle
Ages Masoretic additions were made to scrolls if they had, for some reason,
become unfit for liturgical use. The fact that the leaves of a codex were written on both sides, unlike biblical scrolls, and its overall practical format

---

[5] For the association of the scribal innovations with changes in the physical
form of manuscripts see Khan (1990a).

meant that the entire 24 books of the Bible could be bound together in a single volume, as is the case with the Aleppo codex and St. Petersburg (Leningrad) codex. The less practical scroll format meant that the books of the Bible had to be divided up into a series of separate scrolls. In many cases, however, codices consisted of only sections of the Bible, such as the major divisions of Pentateuch (*Torah*), Prophets (*Nevi'im*) and Writings (*Ketuvim*), or smaller units. Many of these are among those that should be classified as 'popular manuscripts'.

The scrolls generally differed from Masoretic codices not only in the lack of vocalization, accents and Masoretic notes, but also in the addition of ornamental strokes called *taggin* ('crowns') to the Hebrew letters *shin, ʿayin, ṭet, nun, zayin, gimel* and *ṣade*.

The task of writing codices was generally divided between two specialist scribes. The copying of the consonantal text was entrusted to a scribe known as a *sopher*, who also wrote scrolls. The vocalization, accents and Masoretic notes, on the other hand, were generally added by a scribe known as a *naqdan* ('pointer', i.e. vocalizer) or by a Masorete. This reflects the fact that the tradition of transmitting the consonantal text and the tradition of transmitting the Masoretic components were not completely integrated.

So far we have made a distinction between manuscripts of the Hebrew Bible written in scrolls and those written in Masoretic codices and also between the early Tiberian codices datable to before 1100 and later ones. In the early period, coinciding with or close to the time when the Masoretes were active, we can distinguish between various types of Hebrew Bible codices. The type of codex that has been referred to in the preceding discussion is what can be termed a 'model' codex, which was carefully written and accurately preserved the written components of the Tiberian Masoretic tradition. Such manuscripts were generally in the possession of a community, as is shown by their colophons, and were kept in a public place of study and worship for consultation and copying (to produce both codices and scrolls). References to various model codices and their readings are found in the Masoretic notes, e.g. codex Muggah, codex Hilleli, codex Zambuqi and codex Yerushalmi (Ginsburg 1966, 429–433). Sometimes accurately written manuscripts also contain the text of an Aramaic Targum.

In addition to these model Masoretic codices, there existed numerous so-called 'popular' Bible codices, which were generally in the possession of private individuals. These were not written with such precision as the model codices and usually did not include all the written components of the Tiberian Masoretic tradition. Often they contain no accents or Masoretic notes but only vocalization, and this may deviate from the standard Tiberian system of vocalization in a number of details.[6] A conspicuous feature of some popular codices is that they adapt the written consonantal text to make it correspond to the reading tradition more closely. An extreme case of this is represented by a corpus of Hebrew Bible manuscripts that contain an Arabic transcription of the reading tradition. These were used by some Karaite Jews (Hoerning 1889; Khan 1990b). Some popular Bible manuscripts are no more than aide-memoires to the reading tradition, in that they are written in a shorthand form know as *serugin*. In these texts the first word of a verse is written in full, followed by a single letter from each of the other important words in the verse. Some popular Bible manuscripts were accompanied by an Aramaic Targum or an Arabic translation and commentary.

All popular manuscripts were not necessarily written carelessly. The crucial feature of their production was that the scribes felt less bound by tradition than in the copying of the model manuscripts. Many of them are distinguished from the model manuscripts also in their smaller dimensions.

There were, therefore, three classes of Hebrew Bible manuscript in the early Middle Ages: (i) scrolls used for public reading in the liturgy; (ii) model Masoretic codices, the purpose of which was to preserve the full biblical tradition, both the written tradition and the reading tradition; (iii) popular manuscripts that aided individuals in the reading of the text.

We describe here briefly two of the surviving model Tiberian Masoretic codices that have come to be regarded as among the most important and have been used in modern critical editions, viz. the Aleppo codex (tenth century C.E.) and the St. Petersburg codex (dated 1009 C.E.). The latter was formerly known as the Leningrad codex and this term is still commonly used. Both of these manuscripts originate from the Middle East, as do the

---

[6] For this type of medieval manuscript see Goshen-Gottstein (1962, 39ff) and Díez Macho (1971, 22).

vast majority of the early codices. The early eastern manuscripts began to come to the attention of scholars in the nineteenth century, mainly due to the collection of eastern manuscripts assembled by Abraham Firkovitch (1787-1874), the majority of which were donated to what is now the National Library of Russia in St. Petersburg. An important breakthrough was also the discovery of the Cairo Genizah in the late nineteenth century, which contained many fragments of early eastern Bible manuscripts, the majority of which are now in the possession of Cambridge University Library. The earliest surviving codices that were written in Europe are datable to the twelfth century (Beit-Arié et al. 1997). The early medieval codices all reflect a basically uniform Masoretic tradition, though no two manuscripts are completely identical. The differences are sometimes the result of scribal errors and other times due to a slightly different system of marking vocalization or accents that is followed by the *naqdan*.

1. The Aleppo codex

In the colophon of this manuscript it is stated that the Masorete Aharon ben Asher (tenth century C.E.) added the vocalization, accents and Masoretic notes. This is confirmed by comparison with the statements concerning Ben Asher's tradition in the 'Book of Differences' (*Kitāb al-Khilaf*) of Misha'el ben ʿUzziʾel. It is indeed thought to be the manuscript that Maimonides examined when he pronounced that Ben Asher's tradition was superior to that of other Masoretes. It should be regarded, therefore, as the authorized edition in Jewish tradition (Penkower 1981). When Maimonides saw the manuscript, it was kept in Egypt, possibly in the Ben-Ezra synagogue in Fusṭāṭ, which later became famous for its 'Genizah'. From the later Middle Ages, however, it was kept in Aleppo. In 1948 the synagogue in which it was kept in Aleppo was set on fire and only about three-quarters of the original manuscript were preserved. The surviving portions are now kept in Jerusalem in the library of the Ben-Zvi Institute (Shamosh 1987; Friedman 2012; Goshen-Gottstein 1960; Yeivin 1968). It has been published in a facsimile edition by Goshen-Gottstein (1976). This manuscript forms the basis of a number of Israeli editions of the Hebrew Bible, including the *Hebrew University Bible* (Goshen-Gotttstein 1975), the edition of M. Breuer (Jerusalem 1977-1982, re-edited in 1996-1998 with inclusion of new information on

the *parashah* divisions) and the modern Rabbinic Bible (*Ha-Keter*) edited by
M. Cohen (1992–).

2. St. Petersburg (Leningrad), National Library of Russia, Firkovitch I, B 19a.

This codex is still widely known as Codex Leningradensis. The colophon of
the manuscript states that it was written in 1009 and subsequently corrected
'according to the most exact texts of Ben Asher'. It was not, therefore, the
original work of a Masoretic authority, unlike the Aleppo codex, which was
produced directly by the Masorete Aharon ben Asher. The St. Petersburg
codex differs slightly from the Aleppo codex in a few minor details. The
manuscript has been preserved in its entirety and it contains the complete
text of the Bible. Paul Kahle made this the basis of the third edition of *Biblia
Hebraica* (Stuttgart 1929-1937) and it has been used for all subsequent editions. It is also the basis of the edition of the Hebrew Bible by A. Dotan (Tel-
Aviv 1976).[7]

In the Middle Ages Hebrew Bible manuscripts were also written with
systems of vocalization and accents that differed from those of the Tiberian
Masoretic tradition. Some of these systems are adaptations of the Tiberian
system, such as the so-called 'expanded' Tiberian system, which extends
some of the principles found in the standard Tiberian vocalization, such as
the use of the *dagesh* and *ḥateph* signs.[8] Other systems use different sets of
signs. These include the Palestinian and Babylonian systems of vocalization,
which are found in numerous manuscripts from the Middle Ages. There is
no uniformity within the two systems and it is possible to identify a range of

---

[7] A facsimile edition of the manuscript was published by D.S. Loewinger
(1970).

[8] The term 'expanded Tiberian' is the term that is applied to vocalization of
this type by I. Yeivin. Manuscripts with this system used to be thought to reflect
the tradition of the Masorete Ben Naphtali. Subsequently, however, it was recognized that there was no sure basis for this assumption, hence the term
'Pseudo-Ben Naphtali' that was used by A. Díez-Macho to refer to them. Other
terms that have been used for the same manuscripts include 'Palestino-Tiberian'
and 'Fuller Palestinian'.

sub-systems. By the late Middle Ages these systems had been almost completely supplanted in manuscripts by the standard Tiberian Masoretic tradition. An important question is what their status was in relation to the authoritative Tiberian tradition in the Middle Ages. As far as can be established, they both exhibit a convergence with the Tiberian system in the course of their development. The earliest forms of the Palestinian and Babylonian vocalization systems have many features that are independent of the Tiberian system, but gradually the Tiberian tradition exerted its influence and, indeed, some manuscripts are little more than transcriptions of the Tiberian tradition into Babylonian or Palestinian vowel signs.

The model Tiberian codices such as the Aleppo codex and manuscript Firkovitch I, B 19a were kept in the library of synagogues until modern times. The majority of the popular manuscripts from the Middle Ages and the manuscripts with Palestinian and Babylonian vocalization have been preserved mainly in fragmentary form in the Cairo Genizah. This was a repository for worn-out sacred writings that was discovered by scholars in the Ben-Ezra synagogue of al-Fusṭāṭ (Old Cairo) in the nineteenth century.

We shall now examine the background of each of the components of the Tiberian Masoretic tradition.

2. THE CONSONANTAL TEXT

The term 'consonantal text' refers to the Hebrew letters of the biblical text without the vocalization, accents and Masoretic notes. Although this term is widely used in biblical scholarship, it is not completely appropriate as far as the Tiberian Masoretic text is concerned since this consists not only of letters representing consonants but also many letters that represent vowels (known as vowel letters or *matres lectionis*). The use of the vowel letters is not consistent in the Tiberian Masoretic text and their occurrence cannot be reduced to rules. In the ensuing discussion the Masoretic consonantal text is referred to as MCT.

Among the early model Masoretic codices there are only sporadic differences in the consonantal text. They are all in virtual complete agreement with regard to the distribution of the vowel letters. The differences that do occur can usually be explained as an error in copying. Similarly the numerous biblical Masoretic manuscripts written after 1100 only exhibit minute variants in the consonantal text. The collation of hundreds of late medieval manuscripts by Kennicott (1776–1780) and de Rossi (1784–1799) in the eighteenth century showed that the Tiberian text was accurately copied down to the period of the first printed editions. The small deviations in the consonantal text that are found in some of the later manuscripts are likely to be mistakes or intentional changes of late scribes and do not preserve an earlier text that differed from what is found in the earlier model Tiberian codices. It is, nevertheless, possible to distinguish between scribal practices in Sephardi (Spanish, Portuguese and Eastern) manuscripts and those in Ashkenazi (European) manuscripts. The Sephardi manuscripts have, in general, preserved the Tiberian Masoretic text in its minute details of orthography more accurately than the Ashkenazi ones. The accurate transmission of the standard Tiberian consonantal text is found also in the unvocalized scrolls that have been preserved from the Middle Ages.

The accurate transmission of the consonantal text in the late medieval manuscripts should be contrasted with what is found in many of the popular biblical manuscripts of the early Middle Ages which have been discovered in the Cairo Genizah. These frequently exhibit orthographic practices that deviate from what is found in the contemporary model Tiberian codices. In general they use vowel letters far more frequently than is the case in the standard text. Where the *qere* differs from the *ketiv* the popular manuscripts sometimes have the text of the *qere* in the consonantal text.

Early medieval manuscripts with different systems of vocalization generally exhibit the orthography of the standard Tiberian text. Some manuscripts with Palestinian vocalization have a slightly fuller orthography, with more vowel letters than the standard text. This suggests that they were popular manuscripts intended for private use. Manuscripts with Babylonian vocalization, most of which can be assumed to have been written in Iraq, correspond to the Tiberian consonantal text very closely and differ only in a few details. These differences are generally related to orthography, the division of words, or the harmonization of the *ketiv* with the *qere*. Small divergences such as these between the 'Easterners' (*Madinḥaʾe*) and the 'Westerners' (*Maʿarbaʾe*) are mentioned in the Tiberian Masoretic notes and also in lists appended to Tiberian manuscripts.

In the Middle Ages, therefore, we see that there was one authorized consonantal text that was faithfully adhered to by all Jewish communities. A distinction should be made, however, between manuscripts designed for public use that followed the authorized text and manuscripts written for private use that were often less bound by it.

With regard to the ordering of the biblical books, those of the Pentateuch and the Former Prophets were arranged in all manuscripts in a fixed order, but there was a certain amount of variation in the order of books in the Latter Prophets and Writings. The order that is customary today is the one that is used in the first printed editions. The differences from the early printed editions in the Latter Prophets are found mainly in late medieval Ashkenazi manuscripts. The order of the Writings differs from the present custom in the early Masoretic manuscripts such as the Aleppo codex and the Firkovitch I, B 19a. The division of the biblical books into chapters and the numbering of verses that are found in modern printed editions do not derive from Jewish tradition but were transferred from a tradition followed in manuscripts of the Latin Vulgate version that was established in the thirteenth century by Archbishop Stephen Langton in England.

Between the end of the Second Temple period (70 C.E.) and the time of the earliest surviving medieval Masoretic codices (ninth century) very few Bible manuscripts are extant. The codex was not used to write Bibles before the Masoretic period, which began around 700 C.E. As remarked above, it was adopted by the Masoretes as an alternative to the traditional scroll to give them freedom to add vocalization, accents and marginal notes. All extant Bible manuscripts that were written before the earliest attested Masoretic codices are, therefore, scrolls that contain only the consonantal text.

Some biblical scrolls that have been preserved in synagogue libraries and the Cairo Genizah have been dated to the eighth century or earlier (Sirat 1985, 31ff.). Fragments of biblical scrolls have been discovered in the Judaean Desert (Naḥal Ḥever and Wādī Murabbaʿāt) which were written around the beginning of the second century C.E. There are no biblical manuscripts that can be dated to the intervening centuries in the middle of the first millennium C.E.

Despite the passage of hundreds of years the manuscripts from Naḥal Ḥever and Wādī Murabbaʿāt contain a consonantal text that is virtually identical with that of the medieval Masoretic manuscripts, including in details of orthography. It is clear that the consonantal text was copied by scribes with great accuracy from one generation to the next. This concern for precise transmission is reflected in the many rules for writing biblical scrolls that are prescribed in the Babylonian and Palestinian Talmuds. These were collected together shortly after the Talmudic period in the treatise *Massekhet Sepher Torah* and, slightly later, in the more detailed work *Massekhet Sopherim*. Talmudic literature mentions a number of Rabbis who took a close interest in the biblical text.[9] There was an awareness among the Babylonian Rabbis that the most accurate transmission of the text was to be

---

[9] E.g. R. Meir (Palestinian Talmud, *Taʿanit* 1.1, 64a; *Megillah* 4.1, 74d), R. Ḥananel (Palestinian Talmud, *Megillah* 1.11, 71c, d) and R. Shmuel ben Shilat (Palestinian Talmud, *Megillah* 71c, d).

found in Palestine.[10] The careful transmission of the text at the beginning of
the millennium is also reflected by the introduction of rules of biblical her-
meneutics by Hillel the Elder in the first century C.E. and their use by the
Tannaim, since these presuppose the existence of an inviolable, authoritative text. The exegetical importance attached by Rabbi Aqiva (d. 135 C.E.)
to grammatical particles such as את and גם also reflected the stability of the
text.

The many biblical scrolls that were discovered at Qumran provide
abundant evidence for transmission of the consonantal text in the Second
Temple period. These are the earliest surviving biblical manuscripts. The
scrolls are datable to a period ranging from the third century B.C.E. to the
first half of the first century C.E. From the first or second century B.C.E. we
also have the so-called Nash papyrus,[11] which contains the text of the Decalogue. This, however, appears to be a liturgical rather than biblical text.

Some of the Qumran manuscripts, though not necessarily the oldest,
are written in an early type of Hebrew script, close to the Phoenician form
of script that is found in earlier Hebrew epigraphic texts. Most are written in
the so-called 'Assyrian' square script that resembles the medieval scripts in
the basic forms of letters. The Qumran scrolls show us that during this period a multiplicity of consonantal texts were transmitted in manuscripts.

The majority of the scrolls, however, exhibit a text that is very close to
the Masoretic consonantal text, and have been termed 'proto-Masoretic'
manuscripts (Tov 1992, 24ff.). These differ from the medieval manuscripts
only in a few orthographic details and in isolated words. The tradition of the
Masoretic consonantal text, therefore, can be traced back to the earliest surviving Bible manuscripts in the Second Temple period.

---

[10] Babylonian Talmud, *Qiddushin* 30a. This view is also found in medieval
sources, e.g. in the writings of the tenth century Karaite scholar al-Qirqisānī
(Khan 1990c).

[11] This is a single sheet of papyrus which was discovered in Egypt in 1902.
It was purchased from an Egyptian dealer by W.L. Nash, secretary of the Society
of Biblical Archaeology in England and first published by S.A. Cook (1903). It is
now in the possession of Cambridge University Library.

A number of passages in Rabbinic literature refer to the concern of the Jewish authorities in the Second Temple period for the precise copying of biblical manuscripts. The temple employed professional 'correctors' or 're-visers' (*magihim*) to ensure that the text was copied correctly.[12] In the temple court there were model manuscripts, which appear to have contained the standard text that was sanctioned by the Jewish authorities. It is said that once a year all the scrolls of the Pentateuch had to be taken to the temple for revision.[13]

In Talmudic literature there are reports of three scrolls of the Penta-teuch that were found in the Temple court. These differed from one another in small details. They were carefully collated and differences were corrected towards the majority reading.[14] The purpose of this activity is not com-pletely clear. It may have been a means of sanctioning the authorized text against other rival texts.[15] Alternatively, the reports may reflect efforts that were made in the Second Temple period to level variants in texts belonging to the proto-Masoretic tradition. Judging by the extant proto-Masoretic manuscripts from Qumran, there was indeed a slightly higher degree of variation in the proto-Masoretic tradition of the Second Temple period than is found in manuscripts from later periods. Whatever the precise interpreta-tion may be of the Talmudic account of the three scrolls, it is clear that the Jewish authorities recognized an authorized text in the Second Temple pe-riod. It is generally thought that this authorized text is to be identified with the type of text found in the proto-Masoretic manuscripts from Qumran, which was subsequently transmitted with great precision after the destruc-tion of the temple. Some signs of textual collation may indeed be reflected by various marks that appear in the Masoretic consonantal text. These in-clude dots written above, and in one case (Ps. 27.13) also below, certain letters, and inverted *nuns*, which are written before and after Num. 10.35-36 and Ps. 107.23-28. These are editorial marks that were in use in the Second Temple period. They both signify that the items marked should be removed

---

[12] Babylonian Talmud, *Ketubbot* 106a.

[13] Babylonian Talmud, *Moʿed Qaṭan* 18b Rashi.

[14] The sources are discussed in detail by Talmon (1962).

[15] This is Talmon's understanding of the passages (see previous note).

from the text. They appear to have been borrowed from the contemporary Greek school of textual criticism. The inverted *nuns* are, in fact, corruptions of a scribal sign that originally consisted of a reversed Greek *sigma* (Lieberman 1962, 38–46; Tov 1992, 54–57). Indeed it has been argued that the insistence on scribal exactitude in handing down written records in general at this period was partly inspired by the Greek tradition (Lieberman 1962, ibid.).

Before the discovery of the Qumran scrolls, scholars were aware of the existence of texts of the Hebrew Bible that differed in places substantially from the Tiberian consonantal text. These divergent texts were identified in the Samaritan Pentateuch and the reconstructed Vorlage of the Septuagint Greek version. It used to be thought that these texts and the Tiberian Masoretic text constituted three separate recensions. The Samaritan Pentateuch was first made available to scholars when Morinus printed it in 1632 in the Paris Polyglot. The earliest manuscripts are datable to the Middle Ages. They are written in an early type of Hebrew script that resembles the form of script that was in use in the Hasmonean period (second-first century B.C.E.) (Hanson 1964). There is no consensus among scholars as to when the Samaritans seceded from Judaism, though a date some time in the Second Temple period is generally favoured rather than a pre-exilic date which is claimed by the Samaritans themselves. It may have been as late as the second century B.C.E., which would conform with the aforementioned paleographical evidence.

The Samaritan Pentateuch differs from the Tiberian Masoretic consonantal text in a number of respects. In the majority of cases these differences are due to deliberate changes introduced by scribes, reflecting the fact that a freer attitude was taken to the transmission of the text than was the case with the proto-Masoretic and Masoretic text. These scribal interventions include various types of harmonizing alterations that remove internal inconsistencies in content, orthography and grammar. The orthography generally exhibits a more liberal use of vowel letters than is found in the Tiberian consonantal text and the guttural letters are often interchanged, due to their weakening in the reading tradition. Finally various ideological changes have been made, the most conspicuous of which is the substitution of 'Jerusalem' in verses referring to it as the central place of worship by 'Mount Gerizim', which was the centre of the Samaritan cult.

Among the Qumran scrolls scholars have now identified biblical texts that resemble that of the Samaritan Pentateuch. These have been termed 'pre-Samaritan' texts. Broadly, they exhibit the same type of harmonizations in content, spelling and grammar but not the changes motivated by Samaritan ideology. In the Second Temple period, therefore, the pre-Samaritan texts were not specifically associated with the Samaritan religious group. The Samaritans adopted this text for no particular reason, other than, perhaps, on account of it differing from the proto-Masoretic text, which was associated with the central Jewish authorities.

The Septuagint Greek translation of the Bible is an indirect witness to the Hebrew biblical text, yet since its Vorlage differs significantly from the Tiberian Masoretic text in some places, it is of great significance. The name of this translation derives from the tradition (recorded in the apocryphal composition known as the Epistle of Aristeas) that the translation of the Hebrew Pentateuch into Greek was assigned by King Ptolemy II Philadelphus (285-246 B.C.E.) to seventy-two elders in Egypt. The reliability of this tradition is a matter of debate. Some scholars have held that the Septuagint was not the first attempt at translation but a standardization of previous diverse Greek versions.[16] It is now generally agreed, however, that the Septuagint version of the Pentateuch was a single original translation that was made in the third century B.C.E., as is stated in the Epistle of Aristeas. The translation of the rest of the Hebrew Bible was made in the following two centuries. A few papyrus fragments of the Septuagint have been discovered, though the main sources of the text are a number of manuscripts written in Greek uncials dating from the fourth to the tenth century C.E.

There are major difficulties in reconstructing the Hebrew Vorlage of the Septuagint. The majority of apparent divergences between the translation and MCT are likely not to be the result of a different Hebrew Vorlage but rather due to the exegesis of the translator, a concept of etymology different from our own, or corruptions in the transmission of the Greek text.

---

[16] This view was developed by P. Kahle, see especially Kahle (1959).

The style of the translation varies in degrees of literalness. This reflects the approaches of different translators. Some sections are very free and even paraphrases, which makes any certain reconstruction of the Vorlage impossible. Retroversions of the Greek into Hebrew are far safer in the literal sections of the Septuagint. Some of the more certain cases of a reconstructed Vorlage that differs from the Masoretic text include translations that diverge radically from the Masoretic text but can be explained by assuming an interchange of a consonant in the word concerned, e.g. Jud. 23.9 MCT שכר 'drunk', Greek συντετριμμένος 'broken', reconstruction of Vorlage = שבור. The degree of certainty is greater in the transcription of proper names that point to a form in the Hebrew Vorlage that differs from the MCT in one of its letters, e.g. Gen. 10.4 MCT דדנים, Greek Ῥόδιοι, reconstruction: רדנים. Another case where the Vorlage can safely be assumed to differ from MCT is where the translation contains a lengthy addition or omission in comparison with MCT or a different arrangement of material, none of which can reasonably be explained to have arisen by exegesis. This applies, for example, to the book of Jeremiah, the Septuagint version of which is shorter than MCT by one sixth, and also to the books of Joshua and Ezekiel, which contain both omissions and additions relative to MCT.

At Qumran a number of biblical scrolls have been found that contain a text that is closer to the Septuagint than the MCT. The value of these Qumran manuscripts is that they often support reconstructions of the Vorlage of the Septuagint with a text that diverges from MCT.

The Qumran scrolls that have been discussed so far include the proto-Masoretic texts, the pre-Samaritan texts and the texts that are close to the Septuagint. In addition to these there is a group of biblical scrolls that are not closely related to any of these three types of text, but exhibit inconsistent patterns of agreement with all of them as well as significant divergences. These demonstrate that the textual transmission in the Second Temple period took place in a multiplicity of forms and had not been completely reduced to three clearly separate recensions as used to be thought.[17] The

---

[17] This view has been cogently argued by Tov in his *Textual Criticism of the Hebrew Bible* (1992). Before the discovery of the Qumran texts the view of three

proto-Masoretic type of text, nevertheless, was recognized as authoritative in mainstream Judaism and appears to have been the most common one that was in use.

A final category of biblical scroll that is found at Qumran is represented by manuscripts that are written according to what Tov (1992, 107ff.) terms 'Qumran scribal practice'. These are thought to have been produced by a school of scribes that was active at Qumran. Many of the biblical scrolls belonging to the other categories may have been brought to Qumran from elsewhere.

The biblical scrolls written according to Qumran practice do not reflect a tradition of precise and conservative copying but rather exhibit numerous interventions of the scribe. They can be categorized as popular texts that were not bound to the preservation of a textual tradition but adapted to facilitate the reading of the text.[18] The orthography is expanded with the

---

basic text types or recensions (those of the Masoretic text, the Samaritan Pentateuch and the Septuagint) was generally held. A similar approach is reflected by the theory of local textual families, which was first proposed by W.F. Albright (1955) and developed by F.M. Cross in various articles, e.g. Cross (1976). According to this theory, divergent textual developments took place in various local centres (Babylon, Palestine and Egypt) due to the geographical distance between them. A similar view was already expressed by A. Sperber, who held that there was a southern textual tradition (Judah) and a northern one (Ephraim); see Sperber (1940). The theory of local texts of the Hebrew Bible echoes the widely accepted division of the transmission of the New Testament text into different local versions (Palestinian, Antiochian and Egyptian).

[18] For the distinction between model and popular Bible manuscripts in the Second Temple period and parallels to this in the Graeco-Roman world see Kutscher (1979, 77–89). According to Lieberman (1962, 20–27) there were three categories of Bible manuscript in the Second Temple period. These were 'exact copies' (ἠκριβωμένα), which were meticulously transmitted by learned scribes, 'vulgate copies' (κοινότερα), which were widely circulated in the cities for study purposes, and 'inferior copies' (φαυλότερα) found mainly in the hands of uneducated villagers. The distinction between the last two categories is feasible both for Bible manuscripts of this period and also those of the Middle Ages. They cannot be clearly distinguished, however, in the extant manuscripts.

abundant use of vowel letters, which often reflect a different form of morphology from what one finds in the Tiberian Masoretic tradition. The orthography reflects a weakening in the pronunciation of the guttural consonants, which no doubt was caused by the influence of the vernacular language. The scribes also adapted the text when there was a grammatical ir-
regularity (as is found in pre-Samaritan texts).

The Qumran scrolls, therefore, attest to a multiplicity of texts that co-
existed with an authoritative text that had been espoused by the central
Jewish authorities. This variety of texts that is found in Qumran may well
reflect the situation that was found throughout the Jewish communities of
Palestine, though we have, at present, no way of verifying this. It is important to take into account that the sectarian community in Qumran did not
pay allegiance to the mainstream Jewish authorities and so may have felt
less bound by the authoritative text. It may be significant in this regard that
the fragments of biblical scrolls that have been found at Masada and in the
Judaean desert, which were in use by Jews who were loyal to mainstream
Judaism, all contain the authoritative, proto-Masoretic text.

After the destruction of the temple in 70 C.E. the proto-Masoretic text
was the only text tradition that continued to be transmitted in Jewish communities. This was not necessarily due to a concerted effort to eliminate all
other traditions, or, as Kahle claimed, to unify the variant traditions by a
process of official levelling (Kahle 1951). The description of the collation of
the three manuscripts in the temple, nevertheless, suggests that some process of textual unification may have been carried out within the proto-
Masoretic tradition itself during the Second Temple period. The role of a
Jewish council meeting at Jamnia shortly after the destruction of the temple
does not seem to have been as decisive in this matter, as Kahle had held
(Leiman 1976, 120–124; Tov 1992, 195–196). The exclusive transmission of
the proto-Masoretic tradition in Judaism is more likely to be the consequence of historical events. The text of the Septuagint Greek translation was
adopted by Christianity, the pre-Samaritan text by the Samaritans. The
Qumran sectarian community was destroyed. The Pharisaic authorities who
had espoused the proto-Masoretic text as authoritative constituted the only
organized Jewish group that survived (Albrektson 1978; Tov 1992, 195).

The custom of writing popular texts, however, such as the scrolls written according to Qumran practice, in which the scribes felt a degree of freedom from a precise textual tradition, no doubt continued throughout the
first millennium C.E. In Rabbinic literature there are references to readings
deviating from MCT that were found in what is known as the Severus scroll.
This appears to have been a popular text. It was written in the Second Temple period, but continued to be used in the Rabbinic period, having been
donated to the Jews by the Roman emperor Alexander Severus (r. 222-235
C.E.). The readings cited from this manuscript reflect an imprecise copying
with adaptation of orthography to pronunciation. Several biblical citations
in Rabbinic literature reflect slight deviations from the MCT (Aptowitzer
1970), which may also have originated in similar popular manuscripts or
have been quoted imprecisely from memory. In a few cases, the variant
readings of these citations coincide with other known texts from the Second
Temple period. These variant readings, however, were not officially toler-
ated, as is indicated by Rabbi Aqiva's admonition to Rabbi Simeon bar
Yoḥai: 'When you teach your son, teach him from a corrected scroll', imply-
ing the existence of imprecisely copied scrolls (Babylonian Talmud, *Pesaḥim*
112a).

As we have seen, popular biblical manuscripts are found among the
early medieval manuscripts. Many of the Masoretic notes that were incorporated into the Tiberian Masoretic tradition also have the purpose of guarding against the tendencies that are reflected in popular manuscripts, imply-
ing that these tendencies must have existed among some scribes. Apart from
a punctilious attention to orthography, the notes also warn against the harmonization of constructions that are irregular grammatically. The latter type
of notes are introduced by the phrase סבירין 'one may suppose' or סבירין ומטעין
'one may suppose mistakenly', e.g. Jer. 48.45 יָצָא אֵשׁ 'a fire has gone forth',
Masoretic note: ג֗ סבר יָצְאָה 'One of three cases where one may suppose
(wrongly) that the reading should be יָצְאָה (i.e. the gender of אֵשׁ is normally
feminine)'.

In the first millennium C.E. revisions were made of the Septuagint
Greek translation to adapt it to the Hebrew textual tradition that had become exclusive in Judaism. Three of these Greek revisions were collated by
Origen in the middle of the third century C.E. in his Hexapla. This contained
six columns containing the following texts: The consonantal text of the He-

brew Bible, the transliteration of the Hebrew into Greek, the revisions of
Aquila, Symmachus, the Septuagint and in the final column a revision attributed to Theodotion. The Septuagint text in the fifth column was annotated, indicating where it differs from the Hebrew. A later revision of the
Septuagint was made by Lucian, who died in 312 C.E. Since the Greek translation of the Bible served as the official text for Christianity at the beginning
of the first millennium C.E. many Christian translations of the Bible were
made directly from the Greek rather than the Hebrew. The most important
of these is the Old Latin translation (the Vetus Latina), which preserves
many readings of the original Greek translation that have been lost in the
subsequent revisions. All translations that were made directly from the Hebrew in the first millennium are based on the Masoretic text tradition. These
include the Jewish Aramaic Targums (first half of the millennium), the Latin
Vulgate of Jerome (346-420 C.E.), the Jewish Arabic translations (tenth–
eleventh centuries) and the Syriac Peshitta version (first half of the millennium). As was remarked with regard to the Septuagint, however, the Hebrew Vorlage of these translations is often disguised by exegetical render-
ings.

The consonantal text that was incorporated into the Tiberian Masoretic
tradition is a textual tradition that was transmitted with precision since at
least the third century B.C.E., the time of the earliest surviving manuscripts
from the Second Temple period. The history of the consonantal text before
the earliest manuscripts is theoretical. The recent discovery of two minute
silver scrolls from Ketef Hinnom datable to the seventh or sixth century
B.C.E. that contain fragments of the priestly blessing in Num. 6.24-26
(Barkay 1989) do not cast any significantly new light on this issue. Several
general points concerning the earlier history of the text, however, can be
made here.

The extant proto-Masoretic manuscripts show that the text had been
fixed not only in content but also in orthography by the third century B.C.E.
This orthography is broadly uniform across all biblical books, though there
is a slightly greater tendency for using vowel letters in the later books. It
cannot, however, have been the original orthography of all the books that
was used when they were first committed to writing. The composition of the
majority of the books is dated several centuries earlier in the pre-exilic pe-

riod when, judging by extant inscriptions, the orthography was much more defective, with vowel letters used only rarely. It is generally believed that these were written in some form at this earlier period, though the first stages of their composition may have been oral.

Hebrew orthography gradually employed more vowel letters as time progressed. At some stage an attempt was made to impose a standard orthography on the entire text. The slight discrepancies between the early and late books reflect the fact this editorial work did not completely eliminate the original chronological differences in orthography. By comparison with independently attested epigraphic material, scholars have dated the broad profile of the orthographic practices fixed in the proto-Masoretic text to approximately the period 500–300 B.C.E. Some of the later biblical books were actually composed in this period, so it is possible that the MCT orthography in these texts is close to the original.

This was a key period in the formation of the Hebrew Bible as we know it today. It coincided broadly with the canonization of the Pentateuch and the Prophets. The emergence of this concept of a clearly circumscribed canon of sacred literature no doubt was the main factor that motivated concern for the exact preservation of its text (S. Talmon 1970, 166). Some time around this period a change was made in biblical manuscripts from the early Hebrew script to the square script, which was first developed for the writing of Aramaic in the Persian empire. According to Rabbinic tradition it was Ezra who instigated this change of script after the return from the Babylonian exile (Ginsburg 1966, 307; Naveh 1970). Some scholars attribute the fixing of the orthography of the proto-Masoretic text also to the activities of Ezra, who lived some time between the fifth and fourth centuries B.C.E. (Andersen and Forbes 1986, 318–321). Some of the later biblical books may have been originally written in square script. As remarked above, however, the Qumran discoveries show that biblical manuscripts were still being copied in the old Hebrew script several centuries after this reform. Even in some manuscripts that are written in the square script the tetragrammaton continued to be copied in the early script, apparently reflecting a greater scribal conservatism on account of its sanctity.[19]

There are reasons to assume that the biblical text that was fixed for the proto-Masoretic tradition in the second half of the first millennium B.C.E. did not contain the original form of the text.

The MCT contains many difficulties that appear to have arisen by scribal errors in the transmission of the text predating the time in which it was fixed. These errors, which are usually visual, are of various types. They include the incorrect copying of individual letters and words, the false division of words, the conflation of variants and the omission or addition of material. The scribal corruptions must have been present in the manuscripts that were used for establishing the authoritative text. Superior readings are sometimes found in Qumran manuscripts that lie outside this authoritative tradition or in the reconstructed Vorlage of the Septuagint. In some cases, moreover, where two parallel texts from the same source are found in the MCT, one of the texts preserves a superior reading to the other.[20]

The MCT also exhibits various intentional scribal changes to bring the text into line with contemporary linguistic usage, theology and exegesis. It is often difficult, however, to distinguish between changes introduced during the literary recension of the text and those that were made during its trans-

---

[19] Also in early manuscripts of Greek translations of the Hebrew Bible the tetragrammaton is written in Hebrew script, in some cases even in the early type of script (Roberts 1951, 173–174).

[20] Cf. Ringgren (1949). Parallel passages in the Hebrew Bible include the following. Two versions of the same psalm are incorporated in a book of the Former Prophets and the book of Psalms (e.g. 2 Sam. 22 = Ps. 18), in Chronicles and Psalms (e.g. 1 Chron. 16.8–36 = Ps. 105.1–15; 96.1–13, 106.1, 47–48) or in the book of Psalms itself (e.g. Ps. 31.2–4b = 71.1–3; 60.7–14 = 108.8–14). Two or even three parallel passages are found in the Former and Latter Prophets (2 Kings 18.13–20.19 = Isa. 36.1–38.22 = 2 Chron. 32.1–20; 2 Kings 25.1–22 = Jer. 39.1–10 = Jer. 52.4–27; 2 Kings 25.27–30 = Jer. 52.31–34).

mission after the literary growth was complete.[21] The extensive linguistic adaptation of the biblical sources in Chronicles is no doubt attributable to the stage of literary composition, yet the Chronicler may be regarded as both a scribe and an author since he copied earlier texts as well as rewriting sections and composing new ones (Sperber 1966, 476–636; Japhet 1987; Tov 1992, 259–260; Fishbane 1985, 23–88).

Linguistic adaptation sometimes occurred in archaic pre-exilic passages, since some features of their original grammatical structure ceased to be understood in the course of transmission and by the post-exilic period their form had often become transformed and disguised not only in the reading tradition but also sometimes in the orthography by a false division of words. Some insight into the background of these can be gained from comparing the language of earlier North-West Semitic sources, especially those from the second millennium B.C.E., such as Ugaritic and Akkadian texts containing West Semitic elements, for example, the corpus of Akkadian texts from Amarna and Mari. This applies, for example, to an enclitic particle with the form –ma or –mi, which is occasionally inserted between the two components of a genitive construction in the second millennium sources (Moran 1961, 60). Several cases of this evidently occurred in the Hebrew biblical text, but were reinterpreted as plural or dual endings, e.g. מָתְנַיִם קָמָיו 'the loins of his adversaries' (Deut. 33.11).

Despite such adaptation of archaic Hebrew, various linguistic layers are discernible in the Tiberian Masoretic text. Within the corpus of pre-exilic material the major distinction is between the prose texts and certain archaic poetic passages such as the Song of Moses (Exod. 15), the Song of Deborah (Jud. 5), the Blessings of Jacob (Gen. 49), the Blessings of Moses (Deut. 33), the Oracles of Balaam (Num. 23-24) and the Poem of Moses (Deut. 32). The Hebrew of the prose texts was a standardized literary language, which may be designated as Standard Biblical Hebrew. This literary language formed the basis of the literary Hebrew used in the post-exilic books, known as Late

---

[21] Evidence for 'inner-Biblical' exegesis is examined in detail by Fishbane (1985). The majority of the material he discusses, however, relates to the period of literary growth rather than the scribal transmission of an established text.

Biblical Hebrew, which exhibits several differences from Standard Biblical Hebrew, mainly in syntax and lexicon.[22]

An example of a scribal change for theological reasons is the replacement of the name בַּעַל in theophoric names to בֹּשֶׁת 'shame'. The original text with בַּעַל was clearly felt at a later period to be theologically undesirable. In parallel passages between Samuel and Chronicles the original form of name with the element בַּעַל is often retained in the Chronicles passage whereas it has been changed to בֹּשֶׁת in the Samuel parallel, e.g. Saul's fourth son is אֶשְׁבַּעַל in 1 Chron. 8.33 and 9.39 but אִישׁ בֹּשֶׁת in 2 Sam. 2.8ff., 3.8ff., 4.5ff. This indicates that, possibly purely by chance, the manuscripts that were used to establish the proto-Masoretic text of Chronicles preserved an older scribal tradition than the manuscripts of Samuel.[23] The manuscripts used for the text of Samuel, moreover, also contained a relatively large number of unintentional scribal corruptions compared to those used for other books. A scribal change for the sake of euphemism in connection with God may be identified in 2 Sam 12.9: מַדּוּעַ בָּזִיתָ | אֶת־דְּבַר יְהֹוָה 'Why did you despise the word of the Lord?', whereas the Lucianic Greek version appears to have preserved the original text: 'Why did you despise the Lord?'

There are some possible signs of intentional scribal changes that were introduced late in the Second Temple period. The text עִיר הַהֶרֶס 'city of destruction' in Isa 19.18, for example, appears to have been changed from an original עיר החרס 'city of the sun', which referred to Heliopolis. The reading החרס is found in a Qumran manuscript (IQIsᵃ) and is reflected by some of the ancient versions. Heliopolis was the site of the rival temple built by Onias in the first half of the second century B.C.E. and the change of the text to the ominous name 'city of destruction' was apparently instigated by the disapproving Jewish authorities of Jerusalem (Delcor 1968; Kutscher 1979, 116; McCarthy 1981, 238–240). By the Talmudic period a scribal change

---

[22] For these broad historical divisions of Biblical Hebrew see Kutscher (1982, 12) and Sáenz-Badillos (1996, 52).

[23] The view that the standard text of the Hebrew Bible was based, rather haphazardly, on manuscripts that by chance were at hand was expessed already by Nöldeke (1868, 22–25).

had been introduced into the text of Jud. 18.30 by correcting the earlier text 'Moses' to 'Manasseh'. The purpose of this was to avoid the ascription of the erection of an idol to one of the descendants of Moses. This was achieved by inserting a superscribed *nun* after the *mem*: מֹשֶׁ׳ה. Although the reading 'Manasseh' is referred to in Talmudic literature, some of the early versions read 'Moses', e.g. the Vulgate and the Vetus Latina, which, as remarked above, preserves in many places an early form of the Greek version (McCarthy 1981, 225–229). It is no doubt on account of the lateness of the change that the original text was graphically modified rather than replaced.

We should mention here the Rabbinic tradition of the 'corrections of the scribes' (*tiqqune sopherim*). These are places in the Bible in which, according to Rabbinic tradition, the original text was changed by scribes to avoid undesirable expressions in relation to God. One such case is Gen. 18.22: וְאַבְרָהָם עוֹדֶנּוּ עֹמֵד לִפְנֵי יְהוָה 'And Abraham was still standing before God'. Here, according to tradition, the text originally read 'And God was still standing'. The number of *tiqqune sopherim* differs according to the various sources. The *Mekhilta de-R. Yishma'el* to Exod. 15.7 lists eleven cases. Other Midrashim vary between seven and thirteen. Some Masoretic notes refer to as many as eighteen. According to some scholars, they originate in Rabbinic exegesis of the passages concerned as euphemisms rather than in traditions of actual changes to the text. The earlier traditions refer to scripture using a substitute (כִּנָּה הַכָּתוּב 'scripture has modified') rather than scribes changing the text (McCarthy 1981). Another Rabbinic tradition (Babylonian Talmud, *Nedarim* 37b) is that of the *'ittur sopherim*, according to which the scribes removed a letter, usually a conjunctive *waw*, in five places in the Bible, e.g. Gen 18.5 אַחַר תַּעֲבֹרוּ 'Afterwards you may pass on' is said to have originally been ואחר תעברו 'and afterwards you may pass on'. It is not clear what the background of this tradition is and why the five passages in question were singled out. This is especially so since there are many places other than those identified with *'ittur sopherim* tradition where conjunctive *waw* might have been added to a word. The medieval manuscripts, moreover, differ in several other places in the use or omission of the *waw*.

After the fixing of an authoritative text in Judaism, however, the need for theological adaptations and the solution of philological difficulties was increasingly supplied by exegesis of various forms.

Before the time of the fixing of the MCT the various biblical books underwent a long period of literary growth, during which several recensions were often made. The fact that some of the other textual traditions contain texts of biblical books that have a considerably different form from what is found in the MCT has been explained by the theory that these represent texts that stem from different periods of literary growth of the books (Tov 1992, 313ff.). The various parallel passages in the MCT, which appear to have originated in the same source, in many cases exhibit differences between one another. In some cases, as we have seen, this is due to scribal changes, intentional or unintentional, in the transmission of the text. In other cases it reflects the free approach to textual sources that existed during the process of composition and literary growth.

3. THE LAYOUT OF THE TEXT AND THE CODICOLOGICAL FORM OF MANUSCRIPTS

The general principles of text layout in the Tiberian Masoretic codices were largely taken over from the traditional layout of biblical scrolls. The text is written in columns to facilitate reading. In the model Tiberian manuscripts, such as the Aleppo codex or the St. Petersburg codex (Firkovitch I, B 19a), the convention was to write three columns of equal width on each page (see plate 1). According to Rabbinic sources a scroll should have three to eight columns per sheet, which should be wide enough to contain the longest word in the Pentateuch לְמִשְׁפְּחֹתֵיהֶם (Gen. 8.19) on one line.[24]

Some poetical sections, however, had a different layout. These were also taken over from the conventional layout of biblical scrolls. The 'Song of Deborah' (Jud. 5), for example, is written 'space over text and text over space', thus (see plate 3):

The 'Song of Moses' (Deut. 32.1 ff.) is written 'space over space and text over text', thus (see plate 2):

The 'poetic books' (Psalms, Proverbs and Job) have a distinctive layout in two columns with interspersed spaces within the columns (see plate 4). Deviations from the normal column arrangement is also found in a few oth-

---

[24] Babylonian Talmud, *Menaḥot* 30a.

er poetic passages, such as the 'Song of David' (2 Sam. 22) and lists, such as that of the Kings of Canaan conquered by Joshua (Josh. 12.9-24). The lay-out of poetic passages in the Pentateuch is generally of a consistent format in the early Tiberian manuscript codices, with the beginnings of the lines of the passages and also of a few lines before and after them being fixed. The form of the distinctive poetic layout elsewhere, however, is not so strictly fixed (Yeivin 1980, 43–44). The custom of writing the poetic sections of the biblical text in a special stichometric layout can be traced to Rabbinic sources[25] and the Qumran scrolls (Tov 1997a, 147). Modern editors have added poetic layout to many passages in some printed editions that have no basis in the earlier manuscripts.

The Hebrew script of the early Tiberian codices is classified by paleog-raphers as 'Oriental square' script (Beit-Arié 1993, 37–78; Engel 1999, 367–369). This is characterized by erect vertical lines and horizontal lines drawn at right angles to the verticals. Some features of this type of script can al-ready be identified in the Dead Sea Scrolls, but the rigorously perpendicular arrangement of the vertical and horizontal strokes is likely to have been influenced by the Kufic Arabic script, which was used in Qurʾān manuscripts in the East in the ninth–tenth centuries. The Hebrew script was written with a reed pen known as a calamus, as was Arabic script at this period.

The early eastern biblical codices often contained decorations. These included decorative 'carpet pages' consisting of coloured floral designs and also representations of artefacts from Jewish tradition, such as the Ark of the Covenant or a menorah. Eastern manuscripts also include decorative designs formed out of Masoretic notes written in miniscule letters known as micrography. These are found on carpet pages and also in the margin of the text. There is no clear correlation between the decorative form and the con-tents of the Masoretic notes. Decorative sigla of various kinds are also used to highlight divisions in the text, such as the beginning of units of the lec-tionary cycle (*sedarim* and *parashot*—see below) and the half way point of a book (see plate 1). Most these types of decoration appear to have been mod-

---

[25] E.g. Babylonian Talmud, *Megillah* 16b.

eled on parallel types of artistic adorment in medieval Islamic manuscripts (Narkiss 1969).

The model Tiberian codices were on parchment prepared carefully from ritually clean animals. Privately owned 'popular' Bible manuscripts, however, were written either on inferior parchment or on paper, which was adopted as a writing material in Palestine and Egypt in the tenth century.

The later medieval biblical manuscripts from various regions exhibit some codicological differences from the early eastern manuscripts. These include not only small variations in text layout, but also differences in the preparation of the writing material, script form and decorations.

4. THE MARKING OF PARAGRAPHS

The further component of the Tiberian Masoretic tradition is the division of the text into paragraphs according to content. The paragraphs (known as *pisqaʾot* or *parashiyyot*) are of two types: the *parasha petuḥa* ('open paragraph'), which marked major divisions in content, and the *parasha setuma* ('closed paragraph'), which was a sub-division of the *petuḥa*. These differ in the way they are marked. At the beginning of a *petuḥa* paragraph, the first word must be written at the beginning of a new line. If the preceding line ends near the left margin, a whole line is left blank. The beginning of a sub-paragraph (*setuma*) is marked by leaving a space of at least three letters after the preceding text on the same line. If there was not enough room left on the same line the following line was indented (see plates). In late medieval manuscripts and in many printed editions the letter פ is added in the space to mark a *petuḥa*, or the letter ס to mark a *setuma*.

The places where each of these two types of paragraph were marked was a fixed component of the Tiberian Masoretic tradition. Some medieval Bible manuscripts contain lists of the *petuḥa* and *setuma* paragraphs. Similar lists were sometimes written in separate manuscripts. Some variation in paragraph division is found among the medieval manuscripts, though there is general uniformity. Maimonides included in his Mishneh Torah a list of the paragraph divisions in the Pentateuch according to a manuscript of Aharon ben Asher, and by this means sanctioned the Ben Asher stream of Masoretic tradition not only in the marking of paragraphs but in its entirety.[26] As remarked earlier, this led to the adoption of the Ben Asher tradition in Judaism.

The Tiberian Masoretes incorporated the practice of paragraph division from an earlier tradition. It is mentioned in Rabbinic texts from around the

---

[26] Although Maimonides' main concern was to establish the correct division of paragraphs he also recognized that the manuscript as whole was a very reliable model for copyists (Goshen-Gottstein 1960).

third century C.E. The same system of marking divisions starting new lines and leaving spaces is found in the manuscripts from Qumran, both biblical and non-biblical. There is a large degree of agreement between the paragraphing of the Qumran biblical scrolls and that of the medieval manuscripts, which indicates that the tradition can be traced back to the Second Temple period. Some Qumran manuscripts, however, exhibit a type of paragraph division that is not found in the medieval manuscripts, e.g. 1QIsa^a (Oesch 1979). This division into units and sub-units of content is an expression of the exegesis of the text that was applied to it at a certain stage in its transmission.

5. THE ACCENTS

The accent signs are marked above and below the words in the Tiberian Masoretic text. They represent the musical motifs to which the biblical text was chanted in the public reading. This chant gave solemnity to the reading and expressed the sanctity of the text. It also had an exegetical function in two respects. The chant marked the semantic and syntactic connections between words and phrases. It also marked the position of the stress in a word, which can be crucial for understanding the correct meaning, e.g. שָׁבְוּ 'they captured' but שֶָׁבוּ 'they returned'.

One uniform system of accent signs is used throughout the Bible except for the poetic books Job, Proverbs and Psalms, which have a different system. Accent signs are found also in manuscripts with Babylonian and Palestinian vocalization.[27]

The precise musical contour denoted by the various Tiberian accent signs is unknown, yet from a number of sources we can reconstruct their basic pitch and syntactic function. The most important early treatises in this respect are the *Diqduqe ha-Ṭeʿamim* ('The Fine Rules of the Accents' written in Hebrew) by Aharon ben Asher (tenth century C.E.) and the *Hidāyat al-Qāriʾ* ('The Guide for the Reader' written in Arabic) by ʾAbū al-Faraj Hārūn (eleventh century C.E.). It is not clear what relation the surviving cantillation traditions of the various Jewish communities have with the Tiberian system.

The Tiberian accents are divided into 'disjunctives' and 'conjunctives'. The disjunctive accents mark some kind of break in the sense and require the reader to pause slightly. The conjunctive accents are marked on words between the disjunctives, showing that they form part of a phrase ending at the following disjunctive. In the standard Tiberian Masoretic tradition all words that bear a stress are marked with an accent sign. In manuscripts with

---

[27] For the Babylonian system of accents see Spanier (1927) and Shoshany (2003). For the Palestinian system see Revell (1977).

Babylonian and Palestinian vocalization, on the other hand, only disjunctive accents are marked.

All the conjunctive accents express the same degree of syntactic connection whereas the disjunctives express different degrees of pause. For this reason, in the less developed accent systems found in Babylonian and Palestinian manuscripts it was considered more important to mark disjunctives than conjunctives. The two major pausal accents, *silluq* and *ʾatnaḥ*, mark the end and dichotomy of the verse respectively. The division of the biblical text into verses is, in fact, defined by the accent system, a word bearing the *silluq* accent constituting the end of a verse. In most medieval manuscripts scribes also marked the end of a verse by a siglum like a colon consisting of two vertically arranged dots. This siglum, however, is not consistently used in all early medieval manuscripts. In the Aleppo codex, for example, it is not found at the end of every verse.

The two halves of a verse can be split into a hierarchy of smaller units with other disjunctive accents, the pausal value of which can be categorized according to the level of the hierarchy of division that they mark (Yeivin 1980, 172).

The Tiberian Masoretes developed the written accent signs to represent the chant but they did not create the chant itself. The tradition of reading the Bible with musical cantillation can be traced back several centuries before the Masoretic period. There are references to the teaching of biblical cantillation in Talmudic literature. One passage (Babylonian Talmud *Berakhot* 62a) mentions the use of the right hand by the teacher or leader of the congregation to indicate the accents of the reading. The term פסקי טעמים 'stops of the accents', which is found in Talmudic literature, reflects the function of the accents to mark syntactic division. The association of the chant with the interpretation of the meaning of the text was recognized, as is shown by the Talmudic interpretation of Neh. 8.8 '[And they read from the book, from the law of God, clearly;] they gave the sense and (the people) understood the reading' (וְשׂוֹם שֶׂכֶל וַיָּבִינוּ בַּמִּקְרָא), which is said to refer to the reading with accents. Evidence for the division of the biblical text by accents in the Second Temple period is found in a Septuagint manuscript from the second century B.C.E. that has spaces corresponding to the major pausal accents of the Tiberian tradition (Revell 1971).

There is no evidence of the use of written accent signs before the time of the Masoretes. It was the achievement of the Masoretes to create a written notation to record a tradition of cantillation that they received from an earlier period.

As remarked above, the disjunctive accents mark syntactic divisions. Since the syntax could in many cases be interpreted in more than one way, the accents reflect one particular exegesis of the text. In Deut. 26.5, for instance, the disjunctive accent on the first word of the clause אֲרַמִּי אֹבֵד אָבִי indicates that it is syntactically separated from the following word and so the two should be interpreted as subject and predicate rather than noun and attributive adjective. The sense reflected by the accents, therefore, is 'An Aramaean (i.e. Laban) was seeking to destroy my father'. This is a midrashic interpretation, which appears in the Passover Haggadah. Modern versions interpret אֹבֵד as an attributive adjective modifying the preceding noun without taking into account the accents, e.g. Revised Standard Version: 'A wandering Aramaean was my father'.

In Isa. 40.3 the accents mark a major syntactic break after the word קוֹרֵא in the phrase: קוֹל קוֹרֵא בַּמִּדְבָּר פַּנּוּ דֶּרֶךְ יְהוֶה. This indicates that 'in the wilderness' belongs to what follows and the phrase was interpreted as having the sense 'The voice of the one that cries "Prepare in the wilderness the way of the Lord."' The interpretation reflected by the accents generally corresponds to what is found in Rabbinic literature and the Aramaic Targums, which contain elements of early Rabbinic exegesis. The aforementioned interpretation of Deut. 26.5, for instance, is found in Targum Onqelos and also midrashic literature, from where it was incorporated into the Passover liturgy (Haggadah). The traditional Jewish interpretation of the verse is also found in the Latin Vulgate.

A further device in the Tiberian accent system to express the relationship between words in a verse is the *paseq* sign. This is a vertical line that is written in the space between two words. It is marked after a word with a conjunctive accent and indicates that, despite the conjunctive, a slight pause should be made between the two words in question. There are various motivations for marking *paseq*. It is used, for example, to mark a separation between words in a phrase where the reader is liable to confuse them with another phrase, e.g. וַיֹּאמֶר | לֹא 'and he said "no"' (Gen. 18.15), which could be confused with the similar sounding וַיֹּאמֶר לוֹ 'and he said to him'.[28]

There is evidence that in the Second Temple period the exegesis of the syntax of the biblical text did not always correspond to that of the Tiberian accents. This is seen in the Septuagint translation, which often reflects a different syntactic division of the verse. From the Pesher commentaries found in Qumran, moreover, it appears that the delimitation of biblical verses did not always correspond to the placement of the final pausal accent (*silluq*) in the Tiberian tradition. It should be taken into account, however, that, just as there were a large range of consonantal textual traditions at this period, it is likely that there were a variety of exegetical traditions regarding the syntax of the text. This is seen in the case of Isa. 40.3. In the New Testament 'the voice of one crying in the wilderness' of Matt 3.3 reflects an interpretation that is different from the one reflected by the Tiberian accents. In the *Manual of Discipline* from Qumran (IQS 8.13-14), however, the introit 'a voice calls' is omitted and the teacher uses the verse to exhort the sectarians 'to prepare a way in the wilderness', i.e. establish a community there. This shows that the Masoretic interpretation of the syntax was also current at that period. The version found in Matt 3.3 is apparently an exegetical reworking to support the call of John from the wilderness (Fishbane 1988, 367–368). Another case is Deut. 26.5. The interpretation in conformity with the accents 'An Aramaean was seeking to destroy my father' can be traced to the Second Temple period. Midrashic literature, however, indicates that there was also an ancient tradition of interpreting it 'My father is an Aramaean about to perish' (Goldschmidt 1960, 34ff.).[29] It is likely that the exegetical tradition of the Masoretic accents has its origin in the teachings of mainstream Pharisaic Judaism.

As was remarked above, the division of the text into paragraphs (*parashiyyot*) in the Tiberian Masoretic text, which has roots in an ancient tradi-

---

[28] For further details on the use of *paseq* see Yeivin (1980, 216–218).

[29] The Septuagint translation (συρίαν ἀπέβαλεν ὁ πατήρ μου 'my father abandoned Syria') seems to reflect a slightly different consonantal text.

tion, also reflects a division of the text according to the interpretation of its contents. In a number of places, however, the paragraph divisions do not coincide with the end of a verse according to the accents. This is known as *pisqa be-emṣaʿ pasuq* 'a paragraph division within a verse', e.g. Gen. 35.22, 1 Sam. 16.2. The reason for this appears to be that the paragraph division of the written text and the division expressed by the cantillation are two different layers of exegetical tradition which occasionally do not correspond with one another.

Within the accent system itself one can sometimes identify different layers of tradition. One possible example of this is the Decalogue in Exod. 20.13-16. The accentuation of this passage is unusual in that most words have two different accents. The explanation of this double accentuation is apparently that it reflects two layers of tradition. According to one layer of tradition the four commandments are presented in four separate verses, whereas in another they form together one accentual unit.[30]

---

[30] For the existence of different layers of accent systems see M. Cohen (1987).

6. THE VOCALIZATION AND THE READING TRADITION

The next component of the Tiberian Masoretic tradition that we shall con-
sider is the vocalization. This consists of a set of signs that were written below, above and sometimes within the letters of the consonantal text. The
vocalization system includes signs to represent vowels and also signs to represent syllable division (*shewa*), consonant gemination, the distinction between the two types of pronunciation of the so-called *bgdkfat* consonants
(*dagesh*) and the consonantal pronunciation of a letter (*mappiq*). The vocalization notation, in fact, marks more than phonology. It reflects syntactic
divisions in the same way as the accents, in that it marks differences between the pronunciation of words that occur at syntactic pauses and those
that occur within syntactic units. The *dagesh* sign is sometimes used, moreover, in an exegetical function to distinguish meaning. A few isolated cases
of this are found in the Tiberian tradition, e.g. the *dagesh* in the *lamed* of the
word לֹא when collocated with the homophonous word לוֹ, e.g. Prov. 26.17
עֹבֵר מִתְעַבֵּר עַל־רִיב לֹא־לֹו 'he who meddles in a quarrel not his own'.[31] This usage of *dagesh* is more widespread in the Babylonian vocalization.

As is the case with the accent signs, the vocalization signs are a written
notation that was developed by the Masoretes to record a reading tradition.
It is not possible to establish exactly when the vocalization and accent signs
were created. Neither the vocalization signs nor, as we have seen, the accent
signs are mentioned in Talmudic literature or in other sources from the first
half of the first millennium C.E. Jerome (346–420 C.E.) expressly states that
the Jews do not use signs to denote the vowels. In the earliest Masoretic

---

[31] Cf. Yeivin (1980, 49, 294). One may perhaps identify this marking of
dagesh to express a semantic distinction in its occurrence in the prefixes of imperfect consecutive verb forms to distinguish them from imperfect forms with
conjunctive *waw*.

codices datable to the ninth century, however, the notation of the vocalization and accents is fully developed, so the first stages of its development are likely to have taken place at least a century earlier. The earliest indirect reference to vocalization signs is in a statement attributed to Natronai Gaon (ninth century) in the twelfth century liturgical text *Maḥzor Vitry* (ed. Hurwitz 1893, 91). The phenomenon of the creation of a written system to record an orally transmitted reading tradition is a product of the general shift from oral to written transmission in the Middle East at this period.

In the time of the Tiberian Masoretes and also for a certain period after their activities ceased both the Tiberian sign system and the Tiberian reading tradition were regarded as authoritative.[32]

The form of sign system that became standardized represents a fixed stage in the development of the notation. Some extant manuscripts with non-standard Tiberian vocalization preserve more primitive stages of its development and others exhibit more developed stages.[33] In the standard Tiberian system a vestige of a more primitive stage of development can be identified in the vocalization of the *qere* of the tetragrammaton with *shewa* corresponding to the *ḥateph* vowel on the *ʾaleph* in the standard vocalization of the words representing the *qere* (יְהוָה = אֲדֹנָי, יְהֹוָה = אֱלֹהִים).[34] One can compare this to the continuing use of the early Hebrew script to write the tetra-

---

[32] Some of the Masoretes were closely associated with the Jewish authorities, e.g. Pinḥas Rosh ha-Yeshiva ('head of the academy'), who lived in the ninth century. The 'academy' (*yeshiva*) was the central body of Jewish communal authority in Palestine.

[33] For non-standard systems of Tiberian vocalization that represent stages of development different from the one exhibited by the standard system see Khan (1991, 856) and the sources cited there. Some of these used to be thought to be associated with the school of Ben Naphtali, though this is now recognized as ungrounded speculation. The primitive form of vocalization with *shewa* regularly occurring instead of *ḥateph* signs is found in some extant manuscripts.

[34] In some manuscripts with Babylonian vocalization the vocalization of the tetragrammaton has been adapted to correspond to that of the words represented by the *qere* (Yeivin 1985, 912).

grammaton in Qumran manuscripts that are otherwise written in square script (see above).

The other vocalization systems (Babylonian and Palestinian) exhibit various degrees of assimilation to the Tiberian system in the extant manuscripts. The Hebrew grammarians in the tenth and eleventh centuries and also other learned scholars, all followed the Tiberian vocalization, whether they were resident in Palestine, Iraq, North Africa or Spain. The Tiberian vocalization system soon became the standard one and replaced all other systems in the transmission of the Bible. The transmission of the Tiberian reading tradition, on the other hand, soon came to an end. It is not completely clear why this happened. For one or two generations after the last Masoretes, teachers of the Tiberian reading tradition could still be found in Palestine, but not, it seems in all Jewish communities. The Spanish grammarian Ibn Janāḥ (eleventh century) expressed regret that in Spain there were no traditional readers and teachers (ruwāt wa-ʾashāb al-talqīn) with a first hand knowledge of the Tiberian reading.[35] The reading tradition may have become extinct through lack of trained teachers. Whereas the signs of the vocalization system could be copied by any scribe in any community, the oral transmission of the reading which depended on a small circle of teachers could not keep abreast of the large expansion of the transmission of the written Tiberian tradition in manuscripts throughout the Jewish world. As a result, the Tiberian vocalization signs came to be read according to the various local traditions of Hebrew pronunciation, most of them heavily influenced by the vernacular languages of the communities concerned. It is only recently, by studying previously neglected medieval sources, that we have been able to reconstruct the original Tiberian reading tradition (see chapter 10). This does not correspond to the descriptions that are found in modern textbooks of Biblical Hebrew, all of which present a form of pronunciation that was not that of the Tiberian Masoretes.

In a large number of places the reading tradition that is reflected by the vocalization does not correspond to the consonantal text. In the majority of cases the divergence relates to the pronunciation of single vowels in a

---

[35] *Kitāb al-Lumaʿ*, ed. Derenbourg (1886, 322–323).

single word, e.g. 1 Kings 6.16, written מירכותי, read מֵיַרְכְּתֵי 'of the recesses'. Sometimes there is a difference in the whole word, e.g. 2 Kings 20.4, written העיר 'the town', read חָצֵר 'the court' or the division of words, e.g. Ezek. 42.9, written ומתחתה לשכות האלה, read מִתַּחַת הַלְּשָׁכוֹת הָאֵלֶּה 'below these chambers'. In a few isolated cases the discrepancy amounts to omissions or additions of words or phrases, e.g. Jer. 31.38, written הנה ימים, read הִנֵּה יָמִים בָּאִים 'behold the days are coming'. The Masoretes indicated in their marginal notes the places where these discrepancies occurred.[36] In the Masoretic terminology, the reading tradition is referred to as *qere* ('what is read') and the written tradition as *ketiv* ('what is written'). There are approximately fifteen hundred of these notes. Some elements of the consonantal text are regularly read in a way that does not correspond to what is written. These are not marked in the Masoretic notes. The most common word where this occurs is the tetragrammaton יהוה, which is read either as אֲדֹנָי or as אֱלֹהִים. It also applies to the reading of some elements of morphology, such as the 2ms. pronominal suffix, which is written ך- but read ךָ-, with a final vowel, and the 3ms. pronominal suffix on plural nouns, which is written יו- but read יׇ-, without the medial *yod*. The regular discrepancy between the written form of 'Jerusalem' ירושלם and the reading tradition יְרוּשָׁלַם with final -*ayim* is likewise a morphological difference.

There is no uniform trend in the deviations of the reading tradition from the consonantal text. In a few isolated cases the reading tradition replaces possibly offensive words with a euphemism, e.g. 1 Sam. 5.9 *ketiv*: עפלים 'haemorrhoids' (the meaning is not completely certain), *qere*: טְחֹרִים 'tumours'. The avoidance of pronouncing the tetragrammaton, moreover, is presumably theologically motivated. In the vast majority of cases, however, the *qere* does not appear to be an intentional change of the written text.

The most satisfactory explanation for this phenomenon is that the reading was a separate layer of tradition that was closely related to, but never-

---

[36] Several different methods of indicating the discrepancies are found in the early manuscripts; cf. Yeivin (1980, 52–54).

theless independent from, the tradition of the consonantal text.[37] Contrary to a view that is still widely held today, the reading tradition was not a medieval creation of the Masoretes but was an ancient tradition that the Masoretes recorded by their notation system. This tradition had been faithfully passed on orally from teacher to pupil over many generations. There is no evidence that the Masoretes reformed the reading tradition and felt free to introduce exegetical or linguistic innovations of their own.[38]

In the discussion of the history of the reading tradition we should distinguish its textual form from its linguistic form. There is evidence that both of these aspects have ancient roots.

The textual differences between the reading and the written text are referred to in Talmudic literature. Some of the Qumran scrolls from the Second Temple period have in a number of places the text of the Tiberian qere.[39] One may trace back the text of qere forms even further, into the period of literary growth of the biblical books. This is shown by the fact that the ketiv of the text of Chronicles often corresponds to the qere of its earlier biblical source. An example of this is the word מִגְרָשֶׁיהָ 'surrounding pasturelands', which is used in association with the lists of Levitical cities in Josh.

---

[37] Some scholars have argued that the qere and ketiv marginal notes were originally corrections or variant readings that were gathered from one or more other sources, e.g. Orlinsky (1960), Gordis (1971). We take the view here of scholars who have stressed the oral dimension of the text reflected by the vocalization; cf. especially Barr (1968, 194–222; 1981) and Morag (1974). One should mention also H.S. Nyberg who argued that the oral forms of the Hebrew Bible continued to be transmitted after it had been committed to writing; cf. Nyberg (1934). A discrepancy between a reading tradition and the written text similar to the one found in the transmission of the Hebrew Bible is found also in the tradition of reciting the Talmud in the Yemenite Jewish community; Morag (1988). We may compare the transmission of the Qurʾān in which the pronunciation of the reading tradition does not correspond in all cases to the orthography.

[38] The view that the Masoretes were language reformers was held by P. Kahle, see, for example, Kahle (1959). His arguments were convincingly rebutted by Kutscher (1965) and Barr (1968, 214–217).

[39] This is found particularly in 'popular' texts such as 1 QIsᵃ; cf. Kutscher (1979, 519–521).

21 and 1 Chron. 6. The Chronicler is clearly using the text of Josh. 21 as his
literary source. In the original text in Joshua the word is always written as a
singular form but it is read in the reading tradition as a plural: מִגְרָשֶׁהָ. This
reflects a later interpretation of an originally singular form as a plural (Barr
1984). This 'later' interpretation, however, is no later than the consonantal
text of Chronicles, where it is written as a plural. Even if we do not attribute
this interpretation to the author of the Chronicles passage, there are good
grounds for arguing that the text of the reading tradition of Josh. 21 is as
old as the consonantal text of 1 Chron. 6.[40]

The vocalization of some pronominal suffixes offers insight into the
background of the linguistic form of the reading tradition. The *qere* of the
suffixes ךָ-, תָ- and יׇו-, for instance, is reflected by the orthography of the
consonantal text in a few sporadic cases, e.g. יָדְכָה 'your hand' (Exod. 13.16),
גַּרְתָּה 'you have sojourned' (Gen. 21.23), חִצָּו 'his arrows' (Ps. 58.8). The
spellings כה-, תה- and ו- are found also in Qumran manuscripts and Hebrew
epigraphic texts from the first millennium B.C.E. (Cross and Freedman 1952,
53, 66–67; Qimron 1986, 58–60). The spelling of these suffixes with the
normal Masoretic type of orthography is also found in the Qumran and epigraphic texts, suggesting that two different traditions of reading the suffixes
existed. Since these texts come from periods when Hebrew was still a living
language, these differences could also be regarded as dialectal variations of
Hebrew. The spellings כה-, תה- and ו- can be identified with the phonetic
form that the suffixes have in the Tiberian *qere*, viz. -khɔ, -tɔ and -ɔw. The
spellings ךָ-, תָ- and יׇו-, on the other hand, would reflect a pronunciation such
as -ɔkh, -t and -ēw. The readings -ɔkh and -t are the forms of the 2ms. suffixes
in Aramaic, in the Greek transcription of Hebrew of Origen's Hexapla and in
some Sephardi reading traditions of Post-biblical Hebrew (Kutscher 1979,
442–443; Fassberg 1989). It is also found in some pausal forms in the Tiberian reading tradition (e.g. לָךְ, pausal form of לְךָ). The Tiberian *qere*, there-

---

[40] For the antiquity of the reading tradition see the discussion in Barr (1968,
207–222). Cohen (2007) argues that the *qere* variants listed in the Masoretic
notes are linguistic variants that date back to the time of the composition of the
biblical books.

fore, represents forms of the suffixes that are dialectal variants of the forms reflected by the *ketiv*. They are not chronologically later than the *ketiv* forms.

Similar evidence is found in the vocalization of some verbal forms. In Late Biblical Hebrew certain verbs with a reflexive or non-agentive meaning appear as *niphʿal* in the past suffix conjugation form (perfect) whereas they appear as *qal* in Classical Biblical Hebrew. The intranstive form of the verb 'to stumble' (כשל), for example, appears in the *niphʿal* נִכְשַׁל in the book of Daniel (וְנִכְשַׁל 'and he will stumble' Dan. 11.19) but in the *qal* form כָּשַׁל elsewhere. In the prefix conjugation (imperfect), however, the verb is vocalized as a *niphʿal* throughout the Bible. This is because the *ketiv* of the prefix conjugation (יכשל) is ambiguous as to the verbal conjugation and could, in principle, be read as *qal* or *niphʿal*. The Tiberian reading tradition treats the verbal forms as *niphʿal* where this would be compatible with the consonantal text, but the occurrence of the *qal* form in the suffix conjugation in Classical Biblical Hebrew suggests that the verb was originally read as *qal* in all forms. This is clearly the case in the infinitive form of this verb וּבְכָשְׁלוֹ (Prov. 24.17), where the consonant text lacks the initial *he* of the *niphʿal* (הִכָּשֵׁל) and so must have represented the *qal,* but it is nevertheless read as a *niphʿal*. The crucial point is that the replacement of the *qal* by the *niphʿal* is reflected by the consonantal text itself in Late Biblical Hebrew in the book of Daniel. In some cases the evidence for the development of an original *qal* verb into a *niphʿal* form that is independent of the vocalization is found in the Qumran manuscripts from the Second Temple period many centuries before the creation of the vocalization sign system. This applies, for example, to the verb נגש 'to approach'. On account of the assimilation of the initial *nun* in this verb when in contact with the following consonant, the orthography of the prefix conjugation can only be read as *qal* (יִגַּשׁ), since a *niphʿal* reading would require the insertion of *nun* in the consonantal text (יִנָּגֵשׁ). The orthography of the suffix conjugation form (נגש), however, could be read as either *qal* or *niphʿal* and it is the *niphʿal* reading that was adopted in the reading tradition (נִגַּשׁ). In the Qumran text 4Q512 (40–41, 2) the infinitive of this verb appears in the form בהנגשו, which is unambiguously a *niphʿal* (בְּהִנָּגְשׁוֹ) (Ariel 2013, 947). Similar distinctions between the suffix conjugation and prefix conjugation of passive forms are found, whereby the former are vocalized as *puʿal* whereas the latter are vocalized as *niphʿal* (e.g. טֹרַף 'was torn

apart' vs. יִטְרֹף). Furthermore the vocalization interprets certain verbs as *pi'el*,
which are likely to have been originally *qal*. The verb גרשׁ 'to drive out', for
example, is normally vocalized as *pi'el* in the prefix and suffix conjugations
(תְּגָרֵשׁ, גֵּרְשָׁה), in which the orthography is ambiguous between a *qal* or *pi'el*
reading. In the participles, however, where the orthography of *qal* and *pi'el*
would be distinct, the original *qal* is preserved (גֹּרֵשׁ, גְּרוּשָׁה). The shifts of
pu'al to *niph'al* and *qal* to *pi'el* are developments that are attested in Post-
biblical Hebrew already in Second Temple sources.[41]

Another relevant issue in this context is the pronunciation of the letter
שׁ, which is read in the Tiberian reading tradition in two ways, distinguished
in the vocalization by points, namely either as /š/ (*shin*) or as /s/ (*śin*), the
latter being equivalent to the sound of the letter ס (*samekh*). It is clear that
the reading tradition of שׁ differed from the original pronunciation the letter
in the pre-exilic period when Hebrew was first committed to writing, otherwise the letter ס would regularly appear in the orthography where the reading tradition pronounces the sound /s/. It is noteworthy, however, that roots
and words that were regularly spelt with שׁ in pre-exilic books are occasionally spelt with ס in later books, e.g., וְסֹכְרִים 'and they hire' (Ezra 4.5 =
שֹׂכְרִים). Such cases are sporadic and most likely unintentional deviations
from the standard orthography that reflect the interference of contemporary
pronunciation. This orthographic phenomenon can be interpreted in two
ways. The pre-exilic שׁ may have been pronounced as a single sound, presumably /š/, in all contexts. Possible evidence for this is the fact that in the
Samaritan reading tradition the letter is always pronounced /š/, including
where the Tiberian tradition has *śin*. This feature of the Samaritan reading
tradition may have its roots in a type of pronunciation that existed side by
side with the Tiberian type in the Second Temple Period. Alternatively, the
letter שׁ in the pre-exilic orthography may have been intended to represent
two sounds, which, according to this interpretation, are normally thought to

---

[41] For these issues relating to the vocalization of verbal forms see Ginsberg
(1934), Ben-Ḥayyim (1958, 237) and Qimron (1986). For further re-
interpretations of the Masoretic orthography in the Samaritan reading tradition
see Ben-Ḥayyim and Tal (2000, 338–339) and Schorch (2004).

have been /š/ and a lateral sibilant resembling the lateral /ś/ of Modern South Arabian languages. In the Second Temple Period the lateral sibilant would have shifted to /s/. It should be taken into account, furthermore, that both of these alternative types of pronunciation of שׁ may have existed in the pre-exilic period. The necessity to use a single letter to represent two sounds arose from the fact the alphabet used to write Hebrew was in origin the one that was developed to represent Phoenician, in which the two sibilant sounds in question were not distinguished. In Masoretic sources the reading (qere) of the letter שׁ is identified with that of ס, i.e., although the ketiv of שׁ differs from that of ס, in the reading tradition they were considered to be the same letter. This is also the case in Rabbinic literature, in which the qere of שׁ is sometimes referred to as samekh and its ketiv as shin.[42] Here, therefore, we have another case of the qere being datable to the Second Temple Period by orthographic variations internal to the consonantal text.

As remarked, a qere that did not correspond to the ketiv was indicated in the Masoretic notes in the margins of manuscript codices, except in cases where there was a regular discrepancy. In a few cases a qere written in the margin does not differ in its oral form from the reading suggested by the ketiv. This applies, for example, to several instances where the ketiv is לֹו 'to him' and the qere is לֹא 'not' and vice versa, e.g., וְקָם הַבַּיִת אֲשֶׁר־בָּעִיר אֲשֶׁר־לֹא חֹמָה לַצְּמִיתֻת לַקֹּנֶה אֹתוֹ (qere: אֲשֶׁר־לֹו חֹמָה) 'the house that is in a city with a wall (ketiv: a city that is not a wall) shall be made sure in perpetuity to him who bought it' (Lev. 25.30), וְאָמַר | לֹו כִּי עַתָּה תִתֵּן (qere: וְאָמַר | לֹא) 'He would say "No, you must give it now"' (ketiv: 'He would say to him "You must give it now"' (1 Sam. 2.16). The purpose of such marginal notes is to make clear not only the reading of the qere, but also its interpretive content, which differed from that of the ketiv version. In the case of the last example, the interpretation in the qere of lō as a negator within the direct speech is reflected also by the placement of the preceding paseq accent. Another case of a qere note apparently differing only in orthography from the ketiv is וַיִּתְאָו דָּוִיד וַיֹּאמַר (qere: וַיִּתְאָיו דָּוִיד וַיֹּאמַר) 'and David had a longing and said' (1 Chron. 11.17). Here the spelling of the qere note with final יו- -āw (imitating the orthography of the 3ms pronominal suffix) is likely to be a device to ensure that the ending of the word is read as final diphthong (cf. Prov. 23.6; 24.1). A note such as this suggests that the lists of *qere* notes were originally compiled independently of the vocalized text and possibly before the creation of the vocalization signs. References to differences between *qere* and *ketiv* are, in fact, already mentioned in Talmudic literature (Yeivin 1980, §105).

As we have seen, in the Middle Ages various ways of pronouncing Biblical Hebrew are reflected in different systems of vocalization. The Tiberian, Babylonian and Palestinian systems of vocalization not only use different sets of signs but also reflect clearly distinct forms of pronunciation. Indeed within the Babylonian and Palestinian systems one can identify several varieties of pronunciation. In addition to these three traditions of pronunciation, there is the Samaritan tradition, which was not recorded in written notation but has been passed down orally. Although the Tiberian, Babylonian and Palestinian systems differ from one another, it is clear that they are closely related in comparison with Samaritan pronunciation of Hebrew, which is significantly different from all three. We can identify two broad streams of pronunciation tradition, the Samaritan and the non-Samaritan. The close relationship of the Babylonian reading tradition with the Tiberian and Palestinian could be explained as a result of its being transferred from Palestine to Babylonia by Jewish scholars after the Bar-Kochba revolt. These Palestinian scholars also established the first Rabbinic academies in Babylonia at this time. Similarly the official Targums of Onqelos and Jonathan appear to have been transferred from Palestine to Babylonia in the same period (Alexander 1988).

A number of the differences within the non-Samaritan group appear to have arisen by influence of the vernacular languages. This applies especially to the Palestinian pronunciation, which exhibits many features that are characteristic of Aramaic, the vernacular of the Jews for most of the first millennium C.E.[43] A number of Aramaic features can also be identified in the

---

[43] The vowel system of some forms of Palestinian Hebrew pronunciation, for instance, seems to be very close to that of Jewish Palestinian Aramaic, for which see Khan (1997). Texts with Palestinian vocalization also exhibit a number of

Babylonian pronunciation of Hebrew,[44] though it appears that it differed from contemporary vernacular Aramaic in a number of ways and was a conservative tradition. The Tiberian system appears to have been very conservative and was relatively unaffected by vernacular influence.[45] The greater concern for conservatism in the Tiberian and Babylonian traditions is reflected by the fact that a corpus of detailed Masoretic annotations was developed by the Masoretes of Tiberias and Babylonia, but manuscripts with Palestinian vocalization only exhibit sporadic marginal notes, mainly concerning *qere* and *ketiv* (Revell 1977, 238–252). We may compare this to the varying degrees of conservativeness in the transmission of the Aramaic Targums. Targum Onqelos of the Pentateuch preserves a form of literary Aramaic that was used in Palestine at the beginning of the first millennium C.E. The text of this Targum was stable in the Middle Ages and Masoretic notes were developed to ensure its accurate transmission. The so-called Palestinian Targums, on the other hand, reworked earlier Targumic traditions in the vernacular Aramaic of Palestine. Their text was by no means fixed and so no Masoretic notes were developed in association with their transmission.[46] Another feature that reflects the concern for accurate transmission is the fact that the Tiberian Masoretic tradition developed a full system of vocalization,

---

features of Aramaic morphology (Yahalom 1997, introduction). The Aramaic morphological features, however, tend to be restricted to non-biblical texts. This reflects a greater desire to conform to the Tiberian tradition in the reading of the Palestinian biblical texts than in the reading of the non-biblical texts (Khan 2013d).

[44] Examples include the treatment of *ḥet* as a strong consonant, which may reflect its pronunciation as a velar fricative in the eastern Neo-Aramaic dialects. One medieval source attributes to Aramaic vernacular influence the interchange of the vowels *ḥolem* and *ṣere*, which is found in Babylonian pronunciation (cf. al-Qirqisānī, *Kitāb al-ʾAnwār w-al-Marāqib* ed. Nemoy (1939, vol. 2, 140).

[45] According to Ben-David (1957) the divergences between Ben Asher and Ben Naphtali show that within the Tiberian tradition there were different degrees of conservativeness. The transmission of Ben Asher was the most conservative.

[46] For the development of the Jewish Aramaic Targums see Alexander (1988).

in which every word and virtually every letter had its vocalization sign, even if this denoted zero (*shewa*). Manuscripts with Babylonian and Palestinian vowel signs do not exhibit such a consistently full system. This especially applies to Palestinian vocalization, which is generally marked only sporadically on isolated words.

It was no doubt for this reason that in the Middle Ages the Tiberian reading tradition was the preserve of a small number of scholars who had received special training. The Palestinian pronunciation, which was close to that of the Aramaic vernacular, was far more widespread. The Sephardi pronunciation traditions of Hebrew, which are still followed today in many of the Eastern Jewish communities, are derived historically from Palestinian pronunciation. The Babylonian pronunciation, which was also more widespread in the medieval Jewish communities than Tiberian pronunciation, has survived down to the present day in the reading traditions of the Yemenite Jews.

We have already discussed the evidence for the existence in the Second Temple period of certain textual and morphological elements of the Tiberian reading tradition that differ from the consonantal text. The morphological features in the Qumran manuscripts that correspond to the Tiberian reading tradition indicate that these features were not introduced into the reading tradition in the Middle Ages. There is also evidence that the Tiberian reading tradition resisted the influence of the Aramaic vernacular during its transmission in the first millennium C.E. This is seen clearly in the reading tradition of the Aramaic portions of the Bible. In numerous places the reading tradition of Biblical Aramaic reflects a different morphology from that of the consonantal text. This reflects the independence of the two traditions. The Aramaic morphology of the reading tradition, however, is not the same as the morphology of Jewish Palestinian Aramaic, the dialect that was spoken by Jews in Palestine throughout the Byzantine and early Arab period, but has earlier roots (Morrow and Clarke 1986; Fassberg 1989). Jewish Palestinian Aramaic was spoken by the Masoretes during most of the Masoretic period so this is evidence that the Tiberian reading tradition was not influenced by the vernacular speech of its transmitters.

It is not possible to demonstrate the historical depth of Tiberian phonology as a whole. There is evidence, however, for the deep historical roots of certain features. One example that demonstrates the conservative nature of the phonology is the pronunciation of the *pe* in the word אַפַּדְנוֹ 'his palace' (Dan. 11.45). According to medieval sources this was pronounced as an emphatic unaspirated stop, whereas the letter *pe* with *dagesh* in all other places in the reading tradition was pronounced as an aspirated stop (i.e. a stop followed by a short flow of air before the onset of the voicing for the ensuing vowel). The hard pronunciation of the *pe* is also mentioned by Jerome, who states that it is the only 'Latin' *p* in the entire Bible (*p* in Latin was regularly pronounced as an unaspirated stop). The word is in origin a loan from Old Persian. The unaspirated pronunciation of the *pe*, which is uncharacteristic of Hebrew, evidently preserves a feature that existed in the pronunciation of the source language (Steiner 1993). The fact that this feature, which conflicted with normal Hebrew pronunciation, should have been preserved from the original period of composition right down to the period of the Masoretes, centuries after contact of the transmitters of the tradition with the source language had ceased, demonstrates the incredible conservatism of the Tiberian reading tradition. Another feature of Tiberian Hebrew phonology that may reflect conservatism and resistance of vernacular influence is the pronunciation of the *qameṣ*. We know from the medieval sources that Tiberian *qameṣ* (whether long or short) was pronounced as a back rounded vowel. The early vocalized manuscripts of Jewish Palestinian Aramaic indicate that in the Aramaic vernacular of the Jews of medieval Palestine the equivalent of *qameṣ* did not have this quality, but had merged with that of *pataḥ* (Fassberg 1991, 52). In the Babylonian reading tradition *qameṣ* was also pronounced as a back rounded vowel. This likewise appears to be a case of conservatism, since there is evidence that in vernacular Aramaic of medieval Babylonia *qameṣ* did not have this quality.[47]

We have seen that some linguistic features of the Tiberian reading tradition are attested in the Qumran manuscripts. It is important to note, however, that Qumran sources also reflect various features of phonology and

---

[47] Cf. the study of Boyarin (1978). The distinction was finally lost in the Hebrew reading tradition of most of Iraqi Jewry in the late Middle Ages, but is still reflected in Hebrew words preserved in the Jewish Neo-Aramaic dialects of Azerbaijan (Garbell 1964, 98–101) and in Persian speaking Jewish communities.

morphology that are alien to the Tiberian tradition. This applies also to the reading tradition of Hebrew that is reflected by transcriptions of Hebrew words (mainly proper nouns) that are found in the Septuagint. Most of these transcriptions reflect a reading tradition that exhibits significant phonological differences from the Tiberian one. One of the major differences include the preservation in some parts of the Septuagint of the ancient distinction between velar and pharyngal fricatives, as shown by transcriptions such as Γαζα = עַזָּה 'Gaza' and Βααλ = בַּעַל 'Baʻal'; Αχιμελεχ = אֲחִימֶלֶךְ 'Aḥimelekh' and Αναν = חָנָן 'Ḥanan'. In a number of places, moreover, the Septuagint translation reflects a reading tradition that differed textually from the Tiberian tradition, e.g. Isa. 9.7 Tiberian tradition: דָּבָר, Septuagint: θάνατον 'death', which reflects the reading דֶּבֶר. Some of the distinctive linguistic features of the Samaritan tradition can also be traced back to the Second Temple period.[48]

During the Second Temple period, therefore, there were a variety of reading traditions of the Hebrew Bible which differed from one another both linguistically and also textually. The lack of correspondence of some forms of pronunciation with the Tiberian reading tradition should not lead us to conclude that the Tiberian tradition is a later development. There is evidence of the extreme conservatism of the Tiberian tradition and it is likely that a form of pronunciation that is very close to the Tiberian tradition existed in Second Temple times side by side with other traditions of pronunciation. The fact that transcriptions in the Septuagint, for example, often have an *a* vowel in an unstressed closed syllable (e.g. Μαριαμ) where in Tiberian Hebrew it has developed into an *i* (מִרְיָם) should not be interpreted as demonstrating the chronological antecedence of the Septuagint reading tradition, although it may reflect typologically an earlier stage of development. This is shown by the fact that in the medieval Babylonian reading tradition the *a* vowel is often retained in such syllables where Tiberian has *i* (Yeivin 1985, 995ff.). Other examples of typologically earlier forms in the Septuagint transcriptions is the preservation of the original Semitic velar fricatives

---

[48] One such feature is the occurrence of a final vowel on 2pl. pronominal forms: Samaritan -*kimma* 'your (pl.)' : Qumran כמה-.

in forms such as Γαζα (= עַזָּה 'Gaza') and Αχιμελεχ (= אֲחִימֶלֶךְ 'Ahimelekh'), the preservation of the lateral pronunciation of *sin* in Χαλδαιοι (= כַּשְׂדִּים 'Chaldaeans') and proper names with a vocalism that is closer to what is found in Akkadian such as Ορεχ (= אֶרֶךְ, Akkadian: *Urûk*). It is relevant to take into account that in the development of the dialects of a language some dialects may be more conservative of earlier linguistic features than other dialects spoken at the same period.[49] Some features in the transcriptions of the Septuagint and other early sources that differ from Tiberian phonology can, in fact, be explained as the result of influence from the Aramaic vernacular, which was resisted by the standard Tiberian tradition. These include the shifts of short $i > e$ and short $u > o$ in closed unstressed syllables, e.g. Μελχα (מִלְכָּה), Ομμοθ (אָמֹות Num. 25.15) (Kutscher 1968). Likewise, where the Qumran biblical scrolls reflect a different pronunciation from the Tiberian one, it should not be assumed that the Tiberian is a later development. Some Qumran scrolls that are written according to the Qumran scribal practice, for instance, exhibit a weakening of the guttural consonants, whereas these are stable in the Tiberian tradition. It is clear that the Qumran scribes were influenced by vernacular pronunciation whereas the Tiberian tradition is conservative and has preserved the original distinction between the guttural letters.[50]

Similarly, where the reading tradition of the consonantal text reflected by the Septuagint differs textually from the Tiberian it does not necessarily follow that the Septuagint tradition is the original one and the Tiberian is a later development. There is, in fact, considerable textual agreement between

---

[49] Instructive parallels to some of the aforementioned developments in Hebrew pronunciation are found in the Neo-Aramaic dialects. In the Western (Maʿlula group) and Central (Ṭuroyo group) dialects the voiced velar fricative $ġ$ (derived from post-vocalic g) has been preserved. In the North-Eastern dialects, however, it shifted to a pharyngal, as in Tiberian Hebrew, and subsequently, in most cases, was weakened to a laryngal (Tsereteli 1990). For a detailed discussion of this parallel with the history of Hebrew see Khan (2005).

[50] Failure to recognize this led P. Kahle to claim that the Tiberian Masoretes reformed the Hebrew language and restored the gutturals in the Middle Ages under the influence of Arabic; see Kahle (1959).

the vocalization reflected by the Septuagint and the Tiberian one. This
shows that there must have been a large degree of continuity in the reading
tradition. The places where the vocalization adopted by the Septuagint
translator differs from the Tiberian tradition can in some cases be shown to
be the result of uncertainty and conjecture and so the Tiberian vocalization,
although later, would preserve the older, more accurate tradition (Barr
1990; Tov 1984; Tov 1997b, 106–116).

   The precise relationship of the Tiberian tradition with the Babylonian
and Palestinian traditions is not completely clear. There was a complicated
web of relations between the traditions of reading the Hebrew Bible in the
Second Temple period, just as there was between the various forms of the
consonantal text of the Bible. As remarked above, the Babylonian and Palestinian reading traditions are more closely related linguistically to the Tiberian than to the Samaritan, yet some linguistic features of the reading tradition reflected by the Septuagint transcriptions are found in the Babylonian
traditions but not in the Tiberian. These include the aforementioned lack of
attenuation of $a > i$ and also the insertion of an anaptyctic vowel where
Tiberian has silent *shewa* preceding a vocalic *shewa*,[51] e.g. Septuagint:
Ιερεμιας (from where we derive our English form 'Jeremiah'), Tiberian: יִרְמְיָהּ.
Some Qumran manuscripts reflect distinctive linguistic features of both the
Babylonian and Samaritan traditions. For example, many manuscripts written at Qumran according to the 'Qumran practice' exhibit the long forms of
the 2pl. pronominal forms (אתמה, ‏-כמה), which are features of the Samaritan
tradition (*attimma, -kimma*). In the Qumran manuscripts imperfect verbs are
frequently written with *waw* after the second radical where Tiberian has
shewa, e.g. יקטולו, אקטולהו, יקטולהו. Many imperfects with pronominal suffixes
have *waw* after the first radical, e.g. יקוטלהו (Qimron 1986, 50). There are
parallels to these forms in Hebrew texts with Babylonian vocalization, as has
been observed by Yeivin (1972).

   The transcriptions of Hebrew from the first half of the first millennium
C.E. in the works of Josephus, Origen and Jerome, moreover, reflect some

---

[51] For the occurrence of this in the Babylonian tradition see Yeivin (1985,
386ff.).

linguistic features that are found in the medieval Palestinian tradition and others that are distinctive of the Babylonian tradition. Parallels with the Palestinian tradition include the Aramaicizing form of the 2ms. pronominal suffix -*akh*, which is found both in the transcription of Origen's Hexapla and in some manuscripts with Palestinian vocalization (Fassberg 1989). Correspondences with the Babylonian tradition include the lack of attentuation of *a* > *i* in unstressed closed syllables, e.g. Josephus Μαριάμη (= Tiberian מִרְיָם), Jerome *mabsar* (= Tiberian מִבְצָר). The view that these transcriptions reflect dialectal differences from the Tiberian type of pronunciation rather than its direct historical forebear was espoused by Harviainen (1977). Another parallel between these transcriptions and the Babylonian tradition is occurrence of a vowel after the second radical of an imperfect verb with a pronominal suffix where the Tiberian tradition has *shewa*, e.g. Jerome *iezbuleni* (= יִזְבְּלֵנִי Gen. 30.20) (Siegfried 1884, 48; Sperber 1937-1938, 158). In Origen's Hexapla similar forms are found without pronominal suffixes, e.g. ουιερογου (= וְיֶחְרֹּג Ps. 18.46), ιεφφολου (= יִפֹּל Ps. 18.39).

As remarked above, the Tiberian vocalization marks syntactic divisions by distinctive pausal forms of words. In the majority of cases the occurrence of these pausal forms corresponds to the divisions expressed by the accents. In a few cases, however, they conflict with the accents, e.g. in Deut. 6.7:

וְשִׁנַּנְתָּם לְבָנֶיךָ וְדִבַּרְתָּ בָּם בְּשִׁבְתְּךָ בְּבֵיתֶךָ וּבְלֶכְתְּךָ בַדֶּרֶךְ וּבְשָׁכְבְּךָ וּבְקוּמֶךָ:

'and you shall teach them diligently to your children, and shall talk of them, when you sit in your house, and when you walk by the way, and when you lie down, and when you rise'

Here a pausal form occurs on בביתך but according to the accents the major pause should occur on בדרך not on בביתך. Note also Deut. 5.14:

לֹא תַעֲשֶׂה כָל־מְלָאכָה אַתָּה וּבִנְךָ־וּבִתֶּךָ וְעַבְדְּךָ־וַאֲמָתֶךָ

'you shall not do any work, you, or your son, or your daughter, or your manservant, or your maidservant'

Here a pausal form occurs even with a conjunctive accent (וּבְתֶךָ).[52] In Ecc. 10.6 a conflict of a rather different nature occurs between the vocalization and the accents:

נִתַּן הַסֶּכֶל בַּמְּרוֹמִים רַבִּים וַעֲשִׁירִים בַּשֵּׁפֶל יֵשֵׁבוּ׃

The word רַבִּים is normally interpreted as a modifier of the preceding word, e.g. RSV: 'Folly is set in many high places, and the rich sit in a low place'. This is the syntactic division that is reflected by the accents, since the major pausal accent ʾatnaḥ separates רַבִּים from the second clause of the verse. This syntactic phrasing requires the noun 'high places' to be read as indefinite, רַבִּים lacks the definite article. This would have been a possible reading of the consonantal text (בִּמְרוֹמִם). The Tiberian vocalization, however, reflects a reading of 'high places' as definite (בַּמְּרוֹמִם), which would preclude the word רַבִּים from being its modifier and require it to be read as one of the subjects of the following verb: 'great and rich people sit in a low place'.

Cases such as these suggest that the tradition of vocalization and the tradition of accents were independent from each other to some extent. We see, therefore, that the vocalization tradition is a layer of tradition that is not only separate from the consonantal text but also from the accents. So the reading tradition, which includes both vocalization and accents, comprises two separate layers.[53]

The separateness of the reading tradition from the tradition of the consonantal text is reflected in the fact that in the Talmudic period different exegesis was applied to each layer. Some of the Rabbis followed the principle that both the consonantal text and the reading tradition were authoritative sources.[54] Rabbinic literature contains numerous examples of a different

---

[52] For this phenomenon see Revell (1980) and Ben-David (1995).

[53] Even within the accents it is possible to detect different streams of tradition (see above).

[54] This was expressed in the dictum יש אם למסורת ויש אם למקרא 'There is authority in the tradition (of the consonantal text) and there is authority in the reading' (Babylonian Talmud, *Sanhedrin* 4a and elsewhere).

interpretation being made of the two levels of the text.[55] This is also reflected in the Rabbinic form of exegesis that is expressed by the formula *'al
tiqre* ... *'ella* ... 'Do not read ... but ...' In a large proportion of cases this in-
volves reading the consonantal texts with a different vocalization from the
one that is found in the reading tradition, e.g. Gen. 27.27 'Do not read בְּגָדָיו
'his garments' but בֹּגְדָיו 'his traitors'.[56] The motivation behind this practice is
likely to be to express an interpretation of the consonantal text that differs
from the reading tradition rather than to record a variant reading tradition.
It is not clear how far back this exegetical practice can be traced. One
should take it into account, however, when assessing the cases where the
ancient translations reflect a reading of the consonant text with a vocalization that differs from the Tiberian tradition. The fact that in a few cases the
proposed alternative reading in the *'al tiqre* passages corresponds to variant
readings in the ancient versions and Hebrew Qumran scrolls is not necessarily the result of a continuity in textual tradition but may reflect exegetical
parallels.

Another sign of the independence of the reading tradition from the
written transmission is the existence of transcriptions of the reading tradition into other alphabets. We have seen that in the Middle Ages the Karaite
Jews transcribed the reading of the Hebrew Bible into Arabic script. They
also occasionally transcribed the Hebrew of the Mishnah and other Rabbinic
literature, which themselves had an orally transmitted reading tradition, but
never medieval Hebrew texts such as legal texts or Bible commentaries that
had no reading tradition and circulated only in written form (Khan 1992a).
At an earlier period the reading tradition of the Hebrew Bible was represented in Greek transcription. The clearest evidence for this is the second
column of Origen's Hexapla, which contained a full Greek transcription of
the reading of the Hebrew text. From internal evidence it appears that this
transcription was taken from an earlier source datable to no later that the
first century C.E. (Brønno 1943, 460; Janssens 1982, 20–21). Similar tran-

---

[55] Many of these were collected in the work *Midrash ḥaser we-yater*, which is
datable to the ninth or tenth century (ed. Berliner 1872).

[56] Babylonian Talmud, *Sanhedrin* 37a. For a detailed discussion of this practice see McCarthy (1981, 139ff.).

scriptions of the reading tradition may have been used by Greek speaking
Jews in the Second Temple period.[57]

The recitation of the Hebrew Bible in Jewish worship is presented as
an established custom in the New Testament (cf. Luke 4.16ff., Acts 15.21). It
is mentioned by Philo (c. 20 B.C.E.–50 C.E.) and Josephus (first century
C.E.) and is likely to go back several centuries earlier (Perrot 1988). Public
reading of the Pentateuch (or parts of it) is referred to in the Bible (cf. Deut.
31.9-11, Neh. 8.1-8). It can be argued that the very existence of Bible manuscripts implies the contemporary practice of public recitation, since in the
Second Temple period a large proportion of the Jewish population must
have been illiterate (Perrot 1988, 149, 154). The medieval manuscripts reflect divisions of the Pentateuch for the sabbath readings in the synagogue.
In Palestine the custom was to complete the reading of the Pentateuch in
three to three and a half years, resulting in 154 or 167 sections which were
called *sedarim*. The beginning of each of these sections being marked by a ס
sign in the margin (Heinemann 1968). Since the lectionary cycle was some-
what variable in length, the marks of the beginning of the *sedarim* differ in
the extant manuscripts. In Babylonia it was the custom to complete the
reading of the Pentateuch in a single year and divide it into weekly sections
known as *parashot*. These were given a name based on the opening word or
phrase, e.g. בְּרֵאשִׁית (Gen. 1.1), נֹחַ (Gen. 6.9), לֶךְ-לְךָ (Gen. 12.1), etc. There
were originally 53 *parashot*, then subsequently, at a later period, the *parasha*
וַיֵּלֶךְ (Deut. 31.1) was added, resulting in a total of 54. The beginning of the
parashot were marked in the manuscripts by the abbreviation פרש in the
margin. The Babylonian one year cycle became the standard one and replaced the triennial cycle in Palestine. It is the Babylonian one year cycle of
reading that continues in use today.

The marking of weekly reading sections in the manuscripts, however,
did not always correspond to the actual lectionary cycle that was in use in

---

[57] This was argued in particular by F. Wutz, who claimed that the Septuagint translators worked from transcriptions rather than manuscipts in Hebrew
letters; see his paper Wutz (1925a) and, in greater detail, his book (1925b).
There is no direct evidence, however, to substantiate his hypothesis.

the community where the manuscript was produced. The *parashot* division, for example, is found in some early Palestinian manuscripts. Conversely the division of the *sedarim* continued to be marked as a scribal tradition in manuscripts even after Jews in Palestine had adopted the one year cycle (Yeivin 2003, 39).

We have seen that the consonantal text of the Tiberian Masoretic tradition can be traced back into the earliest attested manuscripts from the Second Temple period (third century B.C.E.) and, on the basis of orthography, can be carried back further, possibly to the time of Ezra. Rabbinic traditions concerning the recitation with accents are linked to Ezra (Dotan 1971, 1411). In the introduction to the medieval treatise *Hidāyat al-Qāri'* ('Guide for the Reader'), the transmission of the Tiberian reading tradition is traced back to Ezra (Eldar 1994, 7–8). These statements should, of course, be approached with caution and they cannot be verified. It is clear, however, that the Tiberian reading tradition has ancient roots. When the proto-Masoretic consonantal text was fixed it was already corrupted by scribal errors. It reflected, moreover, literary recensions of some of the biblical books that were different from what is found in other transmissions. In most cases the Tiberian reading tradition has been adapted to the words in the consonantal text that have been corrupted by earlier scribes. The reading tradition, furthermore, although deviating from the consonantal text in some places, does not reflect a radically different literary recension. On these grounds the reading tradition is unlikely to be older than the period in which the proto-Masoretic consonantal text was fixed. This is reflected also by the fact that in parallel passages in the Bible the same consonantal text sometimes has different vocalizations in the reading tradition (Ringgren 1949). A number of linguistic features suggest that the vocalization should not be dated to an earlier period. Some archaic forms of Hebrew morphology that are preserved in the consonantal text, for instance, are harmonized in the vocalization to the standard form, which is reflected by the majority of the consonantal text, e.g. 2 Kings 4.16 *ketiv* אתי (2fs. independent pronoun)—*qere* אַתְּ. Furthermore, judging by North-West Semitic epigraphy from the beginning of the first millennium B.C.E., final case vowels were still in use in Canaanite languages in the period when the earliest biblical passages were composed, but these do not appear in the vocalization. It should be taken into account, however, that some of the later biblical books were probably composed after the process of fixing the proto-Masoretic text had started. Linguistic differences between these compositions and the earlier books are clearly reflected by the consonantal text. There is also some evidence that the historical layering is reflected by differences in the vocalization. In two cases in Chronicles, for example, the *niphʿal* of the verb ילד is vocalized in an unusual way, with *shureq* rather than *ḥolem* and *dagesh* in the middle radical: נוּלְּדוּ 'they were born' (1 Chron. 3.5, 20.8). This morphological feature is not found in the vocalization of the earlier books but is common in Post-biblical Hebrew. The vocalization of these forms apparently reflects a dialectal form of morphology that was current in the time of the Chronicler. By implication, the vocalization of the earlier books must reflect a different, presumably slightly earlier tradition (Morag 1974, 309–310). A further example is the difference in vocalization between אָמְלָל 'feeble' (Ps. 6.3) and הָאֲמֵלָלִים 'the feeble' (Neh. 3.34). The vocalization הָאֲמֵלָלִים in the late biblical book reflects the one that is used in Rabbinic sources (Boyarin 1988, 63–64). One could also include here the unexpected *dagesh* in the *resh* after the particle -שֶׁ *šɛ-* in שֶׁרֹּאשִׁי 'because my head' (Cant. 5.2), which has parallels in the vocalization of medieval manuscripts of Rabbinic Hebrew and in oral reading traditions of the Mishnah (Khan 2013).

Within the vocalization of the earlier books, moreover, there are inconsistencies (e.g. Deut. 5.24 גָּדְלוֹ but Ps. 150.2 גֻּדְלוֹ), which suggest that the reading tradition did not level all linguistic differences by the imposition of a unifying standard, just as some of the original differences in orthography are traceable behind the general attempt at standardization (see above). The linguistic roots of the vocalization of the Bible, therefore, are clearly in the Second Temple period.

Exegetical alterations can be found in the reading tradition, just as they can in the proto-Masoretic consonantal text. Examples of this practice are cases where an original expression of 'seeing the face of God' is changed into the theologically more acceptable 'appearing before God' by reading the verb as a *niphʿal* rather than as a *qal*, e.g. Deut. 16.16 שָׁלוֹשׁ פְּעָמִים | בַּשָּׁנָה יֵרָאֶה כָל־זְכוּרְךָ אֶת־פְּנֵי | יְהוָה אֱלֹהֶיךָ 'Three times a year all your males shall appear before the Lord, your God'. This change is clear where the verb is an infinitive and it lacks the expected initial *he* of the *niphʿal* form in the consonantal text, e.g. Exod. 34.24 בַּעֲלֹתְךָ לֵרָאוֹת אֶת־פְּנֵי יְהוָה אֱלֹהֶיךָ 'When you go up to ap-

pear before the Lord, your God'. This change in the reading tradition is reflected already in the translation of the Septuagint and the Targums, which
demonstrates that it has ancient roots (McCarthy 1981, 197–202).

The proto-Masoretic manuscripts from Qumran exhibit a basically ho-
mogeneous text, but are by no means identical in all details. The text of the
reading tradition that became accepted as the standard can be regarded as
an oral form of a proto-Masoretic text which differed in some details from
the written form that became standardized. The linguistic form (phonology
and morphology) of the reading tradition is likely to represent one of various types that existed in the Second Temple period.

7. THE MASORETIC NOTES

The Tiberian Masoretic tradition included the writing of notes in the margins of the Bible codices. The purpose of these was to ensure the accurate transmission of the text.

The notes belong to various categories. Some of these have been mentioned already in the preceding discussion. The majority relate to the orthography of the consonantal text, with special attention to the use of vowel letters. The orthographical notes are statistical in form, e.g. Amos 9.9 יִפּוֹל, Masoretic note: '(this word occurs) seven times spelled *plene*' (מל ז). One of the most common notes states simply that the form, at least in the orthography in which it occurs, is unique in the Bible (ל = לֵית 'there is no (other form)'). Sometimes the note includes information on closely related forms to avoid confusion, e.g. 1 Chron. 8.6 אֵחוּד, Masoretic note: 'Unique, elsewhere in the Bible אֵהוּד (with *he* not *ḥet*) is used' (ל ושאר קרי אֵהוּד). The notes also give statistical information about the combinations of words, vocalization, accents, and forms that are unusual from the point of view of syntax or spelling. These types of notes are all written in the side margins of the text in abbreviated form (known as the Masorah Parva). In the early Tiberian codices these are written on both sides of the columns on the page, whereas in later manuscripts from Ashkenaz they were restricted to outer margins of the overall page. At the top and bottom of the page further notes are given (known as the Masorah Magna) that elaborate on the abbreviated notes by giving the references by key words to the verses that are included in the statistics (see plates).

In medieval Palestine the reading of the Pentateuch in the liturgy was completed in a three-year cycle. For this purpose the Pentateuch was divided into 154 (according to some traditions 167) weekly portions known as *sedarim*. The beginning of these *sedarim* are marked in the early Tiberian manuscripts from Palestine. In Babylonia the reading of the Pentateuch was completed in a year by dividing it into 54 portions. There is evidence that the custom of the one year cycle of reading also had Palestinian roots (Perrot 1988, 148). This would support the view expressed above that the Baby-

lonian reading tradition is closely related to the Tiberian and Palestinian
ones. In the later Middle Ages the Babylonian practice of a one year cycle of
reading became the standard one in Judaism.

The Masoretic notes contain general statistical information concerning
the number of verses, words and letters in the whole Bible and also the
middle word and the middle letter of books, the Pentateuch and the Bible as
a whole. These were added at the end of the texts concerned, together with
other lists, in what is known as the Masorah finalis. The purpose of this was
to prevent the additions or omissions of words or even letters in the standard text.

Other items that were incorporated into the Masoretic notes include
indications where the *qere* differs from the *ketiv*, the so called *sevirin* (cases
where a different text might be erroneously supposed—see above), differences between 'the Easterners' (Babylonians) and the 'Westerners' (Tiberians) (see above) and differences between various streams in the Tiberian
Masoretic tradition. There are also references to 'corrections of the scribes'
(*tiqqune sopherim*) and 'omission of the scribes' (*ʿiṭṭur sopherim*), which were
incorporated into the Masorah from earlier Talmudic traditions. The references to differences between *qere* and *ketiv* and the gathering of statistical
information concerning the biblical text are also mentioned in Talmudic
literature. According to the Babylonian Talmud (*Qiddushin* 30a) the *sopherim*, the forebears of the Masoretes, acquired their name from the fact
that they counted (Hebrew ספר) all the letters of the Pentateuch. As we have
seen above (n.1) the term מָסֹרֶת was probably originally understood in the
sense of 'counting'. This connection with the Talmudic interpretation of the
term *sopherim* may be more than coincidental, in that מָסֹרֶת may have been
intended originally to refer to the activity of the *sopherim*.[58] Most of the ele-

---

[58] A parallel to this means of preserving the text is found in the early transmission of the Qurʾān. Ḥajjāj ibn Yūsuf, a governor of Iraq (d. 717 C.E.), ordered
that the letters of the Qurʾān be counted and that it be determined at which letter of which word the half way point of the text fell; cf. Ibn ʾAbū Daʾūd al-
Sijistānī, *Kitāb al-Maṣāḥif* (ed. Jeffery 1937, 119). This practice may have been
borrowed from the Jews at that period.

ments of the Masoretic notes, in fact, can be traced back to traditions that predate the Masoretic period. The language of the Masoretic notes is also indicative of their date. The majority are in Jewish Palestinian Aramaic, which was the vernacular of Jews in the Byzantine and early Arab period. A few isolated terms in the notes are in Hebrew. Some of these may be of Mishnaic origin (e.g. פתוחה and סתומה 'open' and 'closed' [paragraphs]), others appear to belong to a late layer of tradition datable to the ninth or early tenth century. At this later period the Masoretes used Hebrew also in independent treatises.

The Masoretic material in early Tiberian Bible codices contains numerous elements originating in the Babylonian Masorah (Ofer 2001, 260–274). This can be explained as a reflection of the migration of Masoretes from East to West.

The Masoretic notes complemented the other components of the Tiberian Masoretic tradition yet already in their earliest attested form in the early Masoretic codices they exhibit signs of independence from the Masoretic text that they were appended to. There were small differences among the early Tiberian Masoretic codices, some having resulted from different subtraditions within the circles of Tiberian Masoretes. In some manuscripts the Masoretic notes relate to readings that do not exist in the biblical text of the manuscript or they contain a mixture of more than one tradition, reflected by differences in readings or differences in terminology. This is the case even in the base manuscript of the BHS edition, the St. Petersburg codex I Firkovitch B19a, which was not the original work of a Masoretic authority, unlike the Aleppo codex, which was produced by the Masorete Aharon ben Asher (Yeivin 1980, 124). This resulted from the fact that in the Masoretic period (ca. eighth–tenth centuries C.E.) the notes existed in lists that were separate from the Bible texts.

The notes were incorporated into a printed edition in full for the first time in the Second Rabbinic Bible edited by Jacob ben Ḥayyim (Bomberg, Venice 1524–1525).

8. MASORETIC TREATISES

Fragments of many independent collections of Masoretic notes have survived from the Middle Ages, most of them in the Cairo Genizah. These contain the Masorah of single books or of larger sections of the Bible. In addition to complete lists of the Masorah, there are lists containing particular subjects, such as *qere* and *ketiv*, the layout of the text into paragraphs (*parašiyyot*), known as *petuḥot* 'open sections' and *setumot* 'closed section', differences between parallel passages, and differences between the Masoretic authorities Ben Asher and Ben Naphtali and between the Easterners (*madinḥaʾe*), i.e., the Babylonian Masoretes, and the Westerners (*maʿarbaʾe*), i.e., the Tiberian Masoretes. Also extant are independent lists of the Babylonian Masorah, which appears to have been earlier than the Tiberian (Yeivin 2003, 97–98; Ofer 2001, 309–567).

The longest independent Tiberian Masoretic compilation is *ʾOkhla we-ʾOkhla*, which contains approximately four hundred Masoretic lists, mostly collating words that differ in small details. The work is named after the first two words of the first list (אָכְלָה 'eating' [1 Sam. 1.9], וְאָכְלָה 'and eat [ms]!' [Gen. 27.19]), which enumerates pairs of words, one occurring with the conjunctive *waw* and the other without it (Frensdorff 1864; Díaz Esteban 1975; Ognibeni 1995). Other lists collate related words that differ in details such as spelling, vocalization, accents and meaning. Several of the lists of the work classify *qere* and *ketiv* differences into a variety of categories. *ʾOkhla we-ʾOkhla* is likely to have taken shape at the time of the formation of the Masoretic notes in the eighth or ninth century. The lists of the work are formulated in Aramaic and they use the formulas and terminology typical of the Masoretic notes. This terminology is in some cases different from what is found at later periods, such as the terms מלרע *milleraʿ* and מלעל *milleʿel*, which refer not only to differences in accent position, but also to the presence or absence of the definite article or to different vowel qualities (Yeivin 1980, 102–103).

A number of early Masoretic treatises written in rhymed Hebrew are extant, mainly at the end of the medieval Tiberian Bible codices. Many of these were published by Baer and Strack (1879). These represent a more advanced stage of systematization of Masoretic material. They relate to selected issues concerning vocalization and accents, particularly the *shewa* and *ga'ya*. In some cases they go beyond description and offer explanatory rules for differences based on their context of occurrence. The distribution of the differing vocalizations of monosyllabic words like בֶּן/בֶּן with *ṣere* or *seghol*, for example, are associated with the occurrence of stress, i.e., when the word has its own accent it has *ṣere* (Baer and Strack 1879, §41). The pronunciation of *shewa* as vocalic in the root אכ"ל is associated with the quality of the following vowel, i.e. it is vocalic in forms where it is followed by *seghol*, e.g., וְעֻגַת שְׂעֹרִים תֹּאכֲלֶנָּה (in the St. Petersburg codex I Firkovitch B19a such mobile *shewas* are marked by adding a *pataḥ* sign to the *shewa*, i.e., by pointing with a *ḥaṭeph pataḥ*) 'and you shall eat it as a barley cake' (Ezek. 4.12) (Baer and Strack 1879, §51). The cases conforming to the rules are collated with exceptions, e.g. a *ṣere* exceptionally occurs in the four cases בֵּן־שִׁשִּׁי 'a sixth son' (Gen. 30.19), בֵּן־אֶחָד 'one son' (1 Sam. 22.20), בֵּן־קָטָן 'a young son' (2 Sam. 9.12), and בֵּן־פָּרִיץ 'son of a robber' (Ezek. 18.10), although they do not have an accent, and *shewa* is silent in אֹכְלֶיהָ 'those who eat it' (Ecc. 5.10), although it is followed by *seghol*. Some of the Hebrew texts gathered by Baer and Strack, furthermore, concern topics relating to grammatical theory, such as the classification of consonants according to their points of articulation, or according to whether they are 'radical' or 'servile' letters, the distinction between construct and absolute forms, the distinction between contextual and pausal forms, and verbal tenses.

Baer and Strack attributed the majority of the texts in their corpus to a Masoretic treatise know as *Diqduqe ha-Teʿamim* (see below for meaning) by the Masorete Aharon ben Asher (tenth century), although they did not clearly delineate the scope of the treatise. Dotan (1967) made a thorough study of such texts and concluded that the original treatise of Ben Asher contained twenty-six sections, which are reproduced in a fixed order in some manuscripts. Other sections, of unknown authorship, were subsequently added to these in various manuscripts. The work was not intended as a systematic collection of rules relating to the accents, but only as a treatment of selected details that were regarded as potentially problematic. This is reflected by the name of the work *Diqduqe ha-Teʿamim*, which can be rendered 'The Fine

Details of the Accents'. Dotan argues that Aharon ben Asher incorporated some of the material of *Diqduqe ha-Ṭeʿamim* from earlier Masoretic collections. This probably explains why the work is in Hebrew, since in the tenth century Masoretic treatises were generally written in Arabic. The source material for the work is likely to have been composed in the ninth century.

Another Hebrew text that emanated from Masoretic circles and should be dated to the ninth century is a list of Hebrew technical terms that are referred to as *Diqduqe ha-Miqra* 'The Detailed Points of Scripture' (Mann 1926; Allony 1964a; Ginsburg 1975, IV 35, col. 2). The text opens with a short introduction that refers to the transmission of the biblical text and its interpretation by hermeneutical methods. This is followed by the list of terms. The terms refer to concepts that can be classified as Masoretic, grammatical, and rhetorical-exegetical. Many of the rhetorical-exegetical terms relate to the relation between the cantillation and the meaning of the text. This demonstrates that within Masoretic circles at this period there was a concern to establish general principles not only with regard to the correct textual transmission and recitation of scripture, but also concerning the analysis of its grammar and certain aspects of the meaning of verses. It should be noted that already in Talmudic times the 'reading' of the Bible did not involve simply pronouncing the letters of the texts, but also having awareness of the sense units that were expressed by the accents in the cantillation (cf. Babylonian Talmud *Nedarim* 37b, where the phrase וַיָּבִינוּ בַמִּקְרָא 'and they understood the reading' [Neh. 8.8] is interpreted as פִּסּוּק טְעָמִים *pissuq teʿamim* 'the division [of the verses] by accents'). Contrary to the claim of Allony, this text was not specifically Karaite (Khan 2000, 18–25).

A number of Arabic Masoretic treatises are extant that are datable to the tenth century. Most of these concern the biblical reading tradition and its phonological principles. In some cases a number of the technical terms and even sections of the text itself are in Hebrew. These Hebrew elements may be regarded as vestiges from the earlier Hebrew tradition of Masoretic treatises. Some of the texts datable to the tenth century include treatises on vowels and the *shewa*, such as those identified by Allony as *Kitāb al-Muṣawwitāt* 'The Book of Vowels' (Allony 1964b) and *Seder has-Simanim* 'The Order of Signs' (Allony 1965). These two treatises offer explanations for the distinction between vowels based on factors such context and placement of stress, and develop many of the topics that are found in the *Diqduqe ha-Teʿamim*. In some cases the explanations for distinctions in vowels is correlated with semantic distinctions, which is a level of functional explanation not found in earlier texts. The distinction, for example, between the forms with *waw* and *yod* in the phrases קְרוּאֵי הָעֵדָה 'leaders of the community' (Num. 1.16) and קְרִיאֵי הָעֵדָה 'leaders of the community' (Num. 26.9) was correlated with a semantic difference relating to time reference, the former being interpreted as leaders in the past and the latter as people who were recently made leaders. The functional concern of the work is also clear in the title of one of the extant sections of the text *ʿilal al-muṣawwitāt* 'the reasons for the vowels' (see Morag 2003, 251–252). An Arabic treatise devoted to the *shewa* that is datable to the tenth century was published by Levy (1936). This develops an analysis of the *shewa* based on a theory of syllable structure. The central concept is that a vocalic *shewa* binds the letter to the syllabic unit of the letter that follows it, whereas a silent *shewa* separates it from the following letter. In the word וְהָאֲחַשְׁדַּרְפְּנִים 'and the satraps' (Est. 9.3), for example, there are four syllabic units, which the author refers to by the Arabic term *maqtaʿ*, viz. וְהָ-אֲחַשְׁ-דַּרְ-פְּנִים. The vocalic *shewa*, therefore, was not considered to form a syllable by itself (see Chapter 10). The treatise warns that mistakes in reading *shewa* can lead to the corruption of the form of words and, in general, has a pedagogical tone. This reflects the fact that the correct transmission of the Tiberian reading still depended on a tradition of teaching even after the details of the Tiberian Masorah had been committed to writing (Eldar 1994, 3–8; Khan 2012, 3–4).

Allony (1973) published a fragment of an Arabic treatise on consonants, which he attributed to ʿEli ben Yehudah ha-Nazir. This also appears to be datable to the tenth century. The extant text is concerned mainly with the pronunciation of the letter *resh*. The author describes how this letter has two different types of pronunciation in Tiberian reading and he establishes the rules that condition the occurrence of each type. The *resh*, therefore, is like the *bgdkpt* letters, which led some earlier scholars before the author's time to combine the *resh* with the *bgdkpt* in a seven letter group *bgdkprt* (cf. Morag 1960). A remarkable feature of this text is the reference by the author to the fact that he undertook fieldwork in the streets of Tiberias to verify his analysis of the *resh* in Tiberian reading, on the grounds that *resh* had

the same pronunciation in the local speech of the (Jewish) inhabitants of
Tiberias: "I spent a long time sitting in the squares of Tiberias and its streets
listening to the speech of the common people, investigating the language
and its principles, seeing whether anything that I had established was over-
turned or any of my opinions proved to be false, in what was uttered with
regard to Hebrew and Aramaic etc., that is the language of the Targum, for
it resembles Hebrew ... and it turned out to be correct and accurate". The
interpretation of this is not completely clear. The Aramaic mentioned by the
author could have been vernacular Aramaic that was still spoken in Tiberias
at the time. The Hebrew must have been the recitation of Hebrew liturgy or
the occurrence of a 'Hebrew component' (Hebrew words and phrases) within vernacular speech. Drory (1988, 33–35) suggested that this report of
fieldwork may have been an imitation of the topos in the medieval Arabic
grammatical literature of verifying grammatical phenomena by carrying out
fieldwork among the Bedouin Arabs, who were deemed to be speakers of
'pure Arabic', the inhabitants of Tiberias being the corresponding tradents of
pure Hebrew. The reference to the two types of *resh* is already found in a
Hebrew treatise in the corpus published by Baer and Strack (1879, §7), in
which, it is likewise stated that this pronunciation existed in the conversa-
tional speech of the common people (והוא קשור בלשונם אם יקראו במקרא ואם
ישיחו בשיחתם והוא בפי האנשים והנשים ובפי הטף 'it is on their tongues, whether
they read the Bible or converse in their conversation, in the mouths of men,
women, and children').

The authorship of these works on Tiberian pronunciation cannot be established with certainty, although Allony, who published many of them,
attributed them to various medieval scholars who are known from other
sources. In most cases there is no decisive evidence for these attributions
and they should be treated with caution (Eldar 1986). It has been argued by
Eldar (1988) that the treatise on the *shewa* published by Levy (1936) and
Kitāb al-Muṣawwitāt 'The Book of Vowels' published by Allony (1964b) are
parts of the same work.

To the tenth century we can also date a Masoretic treatise written in
Arabic by Mishaʾel ben ʿUzziʾel known as *Kitāb al-Khilaf* 'The Book of Differences' (ed. Lipschütz 1965) concerning the differences between the two
foremost Masoretic authorities at the end of the Masoretic period in the first
half of the tenth century, Aharon ben Asher and Moshe ben Naphtali. This

lists disagreements between Ben Asher and Ben Naphtali in 867 specific places and agreements of Ben Asher and Ben Naphtali against another, usually unnamed, authority in 406 places. The majority of the disagreements concern the minor ga'ya (i.e. ga'ya on a short vowel in a closed syllable) and shewa ga'ya (i.e. ga'ya written on shewa) (see Chapter 10). A few relate to spellings, divisions of words, and vocalization. Several of these are listed by Misha'el in the introduction as general differences rather than relating to specific passages, e.g., where Ben Asher vocalized a letter with shewa followed by yod vocalized with ḥireq (e.g., לְיִשְׂרָאֵל 'for Israel'), Ben Naphtali vocalized the first letter with ḥireq with no vowel on the yod (לְיִשְׂרָאֵל); whereas Ben Asher vocalized יְשָׂכָר 'Issachar', Ben Naphtali vocalized this name יִשְׂשָׂכָר (another Masorete, Moshe Moḥe, vocalized it יִשְׂשָׂכָר); Ben Asher vocalized the kaph in all forms of the verb אכ"ל before seghol with ḥateph pataḥ (e.g., תְּאֹכֲלֶנָּה 'you will eat it' [Ezek. 4.12]), reflecting the reading of the shewa as mobile, as is stated also in his Diqduqe ha-Teʿamim (ed. Dotan 1967, §22), whereas Ben Naphtali read the shewa in all such cases as silent. The purpose of the text was to impose a degree of standardization on the Tiberian Masoretic tradition, which had developed into a number of heterogeneous sub-schools by the tenth century, of which those of Ben Asher and Ben Naphtali were regarded as the most authoritative. The readings of Ben Asher in Kitāb al-Khilaf conform very closely to the readings of the Aleppo codex, which was produced by Ben Asher, and also to the St. Petersburg codex I Firkovitch B19a (which contains many erasures and corrections that made the correspondence closer than was originally the case). The Ben Naphtali readings conform closely to the manuscript known as the Cairo Codex of the Prophets (for these manuscripts see Yeivin 1980, 15–21). Misha'el does not give priority to Ben Asher or Ben Naphtali. This lack of ranking of these Masoretic authorities was the practice among Masoretic scholars until the time of Maimonides, who declared Ben Asher to be the most reliable authority. David Qimḥi (d. 1235), it seems, was the first who decided in favour of Ben Asher in the context of reported differences between Ben Asher and Ben Naphtali. A Hebrew translation of Misha'el's list was made by the Byzantine scholar Joseph ha-Qosṭandini in the eleventh century. After the time of Qimḥi many lists of differences between the two Masoretes were compiled, many entries in which were inaccurate.

An important work composed in the eleventh century was the *Hidāyat al-Qāriʾ* 'The Guide for the Reader'. This work was studied in detail by Eldar, who published long sections of it (see, in particular, Eldar 1994 and the references cited there). It can be classified as a Masoretic treatise, although, unlike the treatises discussed above, the *Hidāyat al-Qāriʾ* was composed a considerable time (roughly a century) after the time of the final Tiberian Masoretic authorities, Ben Asher and Ben Naphtali. Its author was the Karaite grammarian ʾAbū al-Faraj Hārūn, who was active in Jerusalem in the first half of the eleventh century (see Chapter 9). Although he did not have direct contact with the Masoretes of the tenth century, he did have access to teachers of the Tiberian reading tradition, who could still be found in Palestine in the eleventh century, in addition to the Masoretic treatises of earlier generations. ʾAbū al-Faraj produced the work in a long and a short version. The long version, which was composed first, contains more expansive theoretical discussions. The short version became more popular, as is reflected by the greater number of extant manuscripts. The work presents a systematic description of the consonants, vowels (including *shewa*), and accents. It was divided into two parts, part one being devoted to the consonants and vowels, and part two to the accents. The *Hidāyat al-Qāriʾ* was conveyed beyond the confines of Palestine to Yemen and to Europe. The long version was transmitted to Yemen it seems in the thirteenth century. Two abridgements were made of this in Yemen, one in Arabic (ed. Neubauer 1891) and one in Hebrew (ed. Derenbourg 1871). Each of these was known as *Maḥberet ha-Tījān* 'The Composition of the Crowns', since they were copied at the beginning of Bible codices known as 'crowns' (Arabic *tījān*) (Eldar 1994, 15–16). The short version of *Hidāyat al-Qāriʾ* found its way to central Europe and two full Hebrew translations were made of it. One was made in Mainz and was given the title *Horayat ha-Qore* 'Guide for the Reader' in the manuscripts, the earliest being datable to the thirteenth century. The other translation was given the title *Tokhen ʿEzra* 'The Ruling of Ezra' in a manuscript dated 1145 and the title *Ṭaʿame ha-Miqra* 'The Accents of the Bible' in a manuscript dated 1285–1287. Both copies were made in Italy. In the version entitled *Ṭaʿame ha-Miqra* the work is erroneously attributed to the Spanish grammarian Yehuda ibn Balʿam (Busi 1984; Eldar 1994, 16–18).

9. MASORAH AND GRAMMAR

The rudiments of grammatical analysis are found in the Masoretic notes (Dotan 1990) and some Masoretic texts that are appended to Bible manuscripts.[59] By the tenth century independent treatises of a grammatical nature began to be written in the East. These can be classified into the works of Saadya Gaon and the works of the Karaite grammarians. The grammatical writings of Saadya contain elements taken from the Masoretic tradition (Dotan 1997). After leaving Egypt, Saadya spent a few years in Tiberias studying among the Masoretes. According to Dotan he composed his main grammar book (*Kitāb Fasīḥ Luġat al-ʿIbrāniyyīn* 'The Book of the Eloquence of the Language of the Hebrews) while he was in Tiberias during the second decade of the tenth century. The surviving sections of the work include not only treatments of grammatical inflection and word structure, but also several chapters relating to the Tiberian reading tradition. The material for some of these has clearly been incorporated from the Masoretic tradition and direct parallels can be found in the extant Masoretic treatises, such as *Diqduqe ha-Teʿamim* (Dotan 1997, 34–36). Dotan, indeed, suggests that one of the missing chapters may have been concerned specifically with accents. We may say that Saadya's grammar book is not a product of collaboration with the Masoretes or a complementary expansion of the scope of Masoretic teaching, but rather was intended to stand apart from the Masoretic tradition.

The Karaite grammatical texts, on the other hand, reflect a closer association with Masoretic activities, in that they were intended to complement the Masoretic treatises rather than incorporate elements from them. The tradition of Karaite grammatical thought originated in Iran and Iraq in the tenth century (Khan 2003). The most important surviving Karaite grammatical treatise from the early period is the *Diqduq* of ʾAbū Yaʿqūb Yūsuf Ibn Nūḥ, who migrated to Jerusalem from Iraq (Khan 2000). As has already

---

[59] E.g. many of the texts published in Baer and Strack (Baer and Strack 1879).

been remarked, several elements of the Masoretic material in Tiberian Bible codices have their origin in the Babylonian (Iraqi) tradition (Ofer 2001, 260–274). The *Diqduq* of Ibn Nūḥ is a series of grammatical notes on the Bible written in Judaeo-Arabic. It is not a systematic grammatical description but rather is largely concerned with the formulation of grammatical rules that account for the occurrence of fine distinctions in the morphological form of words. This had its parallel in the methodology of collating words differing in small details in the Masoretic notes and Masoretic treatises. In the class of verbs which we refer to as final geminates, for example, there is variation in the position of stress in the past forms, e.g. קַלּוּ (Job 9.25) vs. וְקַלּוּ (Hab. 1.8). According to Ibn Nūḥ this is not an arbitrary variation, but rather the forms with the penultimate stress are derived from a noun base whereas the forms with final stress have a verbal imperative base.[60] The term *Diqduq* in the title of the work has the sense of the investigation of the fine points (of linguistic form). The *Diqduq* of Ibn Nūḥ contains some discussion of pronunciation and accents, but this is usually related to some issue regarding linguistic form. The *Diqduq* was intended, it seems, to complement such treatises as *Diqduqe ha-Teʿamim*, the exclusive concern of which was pronunciation and accents.

The grammatical activity denoted by the term *diqduq* in the early Karaite tradition, therefore, was closely associated with the work of the Tiberian Masoretes. This is further shown by an early text published by Allony (1964) that contains a list of technical terms for the various aspects of biblical study. These are described in the text as *diqduqe ha-miqra*, which has the sense of 'the fine points of scripture established by detailed investigation'. The list includes masoretic, grammatical and hermeneutical terms. These correspond closely to the terminology and concepts of Ibn Nūḥ's *Diqduq*. The range of the topics of analysis denoted by the terms also parallels the scope of analysis that is found in the *Diqduq*, though, as we have remarked, the focus of the *Diqduq* is more on the grammatical and hermeneutical aspects than on the Masoretic. It is more accurate to say that the Masoretic works and Ibn Nūḥ's *Diqduq* combined cover the range of topics contained in the

---

[60] For details see Khan (2000).

list. The Masorah and the grammatical work of Ibn Nūḥ complement each other to establish the *diqduqe ha-miqra*. This list was not intended primarily as a foundation for the study of grammar per se, but rather as a methodology for establishing the correct interpretation of scripture.

Allony, in his edition of this list of technical terms, claimed that it was of Karaite background. One should be cautious, however, of being too categorical on this issue. Certain details of its content suggest that it was composed in the early Islamic period. It would, therefore, come from a period when Karaism was in its embryonic stages of development. The main evidence that Allony cites for its being a Karaite work is the reference in the text to the 'masters of Bible study' (*baʿale ha-miqra*). This term was used in some texts in the Middle Ages to designate Karaites.[61] It is found, however, already in Rabbinic literature in the sense of 'those who study only the Bible and not the Mishnah or Gemara'.[62] It should be noted, moreover, that in Masoretic texts it is sometimes used as an epithet of the Masoretes, who were professionally occupied with the investigation of the Bible.[63] The contents of the list were incorporated by a number of later authors into their works. These included not only Karaites but also Rabbanites, such as Dunash ben Labraṭ.[64]

The fact that some of the grammatical terms found in Ibn Nūḥ's *Diqduq* are Hebrew is significant for the dating of the origins of the Karaite grammatical tradition. The list of *diqduqe ha-miqra* is entirely in Hebrew. This is in conformity with the use of Hebrew in Masoretic works before the tenth century. The Hebrew technical terms of Ibn Nūḥ's *Diqduq* would be vestiges from this early period. Some of this Hebrew terminology can, in fact, be traced to Rabbinic texts.[65] It is clear, however, that the Karaite grammatical tradition also took over elements from Arabic grammatical thought. The

---

[61] It is used frequently in this way by the Karaites Salmon ben Yeruḥam and Judah Hadassi.

[62] Cf. Bacher (1899, 118).

[63] E.g. Baer and Strack (1879, xxxviii).

[64] *Teshuvot* (ed. Sáenz-Badillos 1980, 15*).

[65] See Bacher (1974, 4; 1899, 99–100), Yeivin (1980, 116), Dotan (1990, 27–28).

Diqduq of Ibn Nūḥ contains some Arabic technical terms. Moreover, many of the Hebrew terms that are found in the list of *diqduqe ha-miqra* and also in Ibn Nūḥ's *Diqduq* appear to be calques of Arabic terminology. R. Talmon (1998) has shown that some of the Arabic terms that correspond to the Hebrew of the list *diqduqe ha-miqra* are found in the earliest layers of the tradition of Arabic grammar and Qurʾānic exegesis in the eighth and ninth centuries. This early tradition differed from the tradition based on the teachings of Sībawayhi, which became the mainstream school in Arabic grammar after the ninth century. It is relevant to note that Arabic grammatical thought in its early stages was closely associated with Qurʾānic exegesis and only later became a distinct discipline.[66] This would parallel the association between grammar and exegesis reflected by the *diqduqe ha-miqra* list and also the fact that the *Diqduq* of Ibn Nūḥ has the structure of a biblical commentary rather than a systematic description of grammar.

The *diqduqe ha-miqra* list and the Masoretic treatises such as *Diqduqe ha-Ṭeʿamim* belong to the Tiberian Masoretic tradition. It should be noted, however, that the Karaite grammatical tradition had its roots in the East in Iraq and Iran rather than in Palestine (Khan 2003). This reflects the fact that the Tiberian Masoretic tradition was not restricted to a local diffusion but rather was regarded as a prestigious tradition by Jewish scholars, Rabbanite and Karaite, throughout the Near East. The Karaite al-Qirqisānī writing in the first half of the tenth century in Iraq explicitly states the superiority of the Tiberian tradition (Khan 1990c). There are references in medieval sources to the fact that scholars from Tiberias travelled long distances to teach the Tiberian tradition.[67] Moreover, scholars from the eastern communities of Iraq and Iran came into contact with the Tiberian Masoretes by migration to Palestine. This applied to numerous Karaites, including Yūsuf ibn Nūḥ himself. As remarked already, the Masoretic material in early Tiberian Bible codices contains numerous elements originating in the Babylonian Masorah (Ofer 2001, 260–274). This can be explained as a reflection of the migration of Masoretes from East to West.

---

[66] See Versteegh (1993).

[67] See Khan (1990c) for details.

In the eleventh century the Karaite grammarian ʾAbū al-Faraj Hārūn ibn Faraj, who, like Ibn Nūḥ was based in Jerusalem, wrote several works on the Hebrew language. The largest of these is a comprehensive work on Hebrew morphology and syntax consisting of eight parts entitled *al-Kitāb al-Muštamil ʿalā al-ʾUṣūl wa-l-Fuṣūl fī al-Luġa al-ʿIbrāniyya* 'The Comprehensive Book of General Principles and Particular Rules of the Hebrew Language' (Bacher 1895, Khan 2003). He subsequently produced a shorter version of this called *al-Kitāb al-Kāfī* 'The Sufficient Book' (Khan, Gallego and Olszowy-Schlanger 2003). The works of ʾAbū al-Faraj were radically different from the *Diqduq* of Ibn Nūḥ in their approach. This was because ʾAbū al-Faraj systematically applied to Hebrew the theories of grammar that had been developed by the Baṣran school of Arabic grammarians. The teachings of the Baṣran school had become the mainstream tradition of Arabic grammatical thought by that period. There was, nevertheless, a certain degree of continuity of grammatical thought from the teachings of the earlier Karaite grammarians in the works of ʾAbū al-Faraj, which can be found especially in some of his theories of morphological structure. This continuity can be identified also in the scope of his grammatical works and their complementarity to the Masoretic treatises. The subject matter of *al-Kitāb al-Muštamil* and his other grammatical works includes mainly the description of morphology and syntax. There is no systematic description of pronunciation or the accents. As we have seen, ʾAbū al-Faraj devoted a separate work to this topic, viz. the *Hidāyat al-Qāriʾ* 'The Guide for the Reader'. This was intended by him to complement his work on grammar. It was conceived as a continuity of earlier Masoretic treatises on pronunciation and accents, which were among his sources, as ʾAbū al-Faraj states in his introduction to the work. Thus the composition of *Hidāyat al-Qāri* by ʾAbū al-Faraj separately from his grammatical works may be explained as a continuation of the complementarity between grammatical and Masoretic treatises that existed among the Karaite grammarians of the previous generation.

10. THE TIBERIAN PRONUNCIATION TRADITION

The Tiberian pronunciation of Hebrew can be reconstructed on the basis of a variety of medieval sources, the most important of which are (i) early Tiberian Masoretic manuscripts, (ii) Masoretic and Eastern grammatical texts, especially the work *Hidāyat al-Qāriʾ* 'Guide for the Reader' by the eleventh-century Karaite grammarian ʾAbū al-Faraj Hārūn (Eldar 1994), (iii) transcriptions of the Hebrew Bible into Arabic script by Karaite scribes (Khan 1990b; Khan 1992a), and (iv) Judaeo-Arabic texts with Tiberian vocalization (Khan 1992b; Khan 2010). The following description of the Tiberian pronunciation relies on these sources.

10.1. Consonants

Most consonants in the Tiberian vocalization are written with or without *dagesh*. In the laryngals, pharyngals and *resh*, however, *dagesh* is not written, except in a few isolated cases. In some manuscripts consonants that do not contain *dagesh* have a horizontal line written over them known as *raphe*. The *dagesh* sign was used mainly in two contexts. These are (i) on a consonant that was geminated and (ii) on the consonants *bgdkpt* when they were realized as plosives. In both cases the letter with *dagesh* was pronounced with greater pressure than its counterpart without *dagesh*. It is this increased pressure, common to both, that the Masoretes marked. They did not explicitly mark consonant gemination but only increased muscular pressure, which is a component of gemination.

Dagesh was pronounced with varying degrees of strength. The medieval sources distinguish three different degrees. These are usually referred to in connection with the word בָּתִּים [bɔːttiːm] 'houses', in which the letter ת *taw* was said to have been pronounced weaker than in the word בַּתִּים [battiːm] 'baths (units of measure)'. In some circumstances, however, the strength of the *dagesh* in the letter ת *taw* of בָּתִּים [bɔːttiːm] 'houses' was intermediate between the one heard in the normal pronunciation of this word and the

one in the word בָּתִּים. According to the Masorete Ben Naphtali this intermediate strength of *dagesh* occurred in all cases of בָּתִּים with a secondary accent
on the first syllable. According to Ben Asher the intermediate articulation
applies only in two cases where there was a secondary accent, viz. וּבָתִּים
[uvɔːttiːm] (Deut. 6.11) and בָּתֵּיו [bɔːttɔːv] (1 Chron. 28.11), both of which
have the accents *qadma* and *'azla*.[68] The *dagesh* sign is occasionally used to
distinguish meaning; for example, the *dagesh* in the *lamed* of the word לֹא
when collocated with the homophonous word לֹו, e.g. Prov. 26.17 לֹּא־לֹו [lloː
loː] (Yeivin 1980, 49, 294).

'Aleph (א) /ʔ/:

Glottal plosive [ʔ].

'Aleph takes *dagesh* in four words in the standard Tiberian vocalization tradition: וַיָּבִיאּוּ לֹו [vajjɔːviːʔuː loː] 'and they brought to him' (Gen. 43.26), וַיָּבִיאּוּ
לָּנוּ [vajjɔːviːʔuː lɔːnuː] 'and they brought to us' (Ezra 8.18), תָּבִיאּוּ [tɔːviːʔuː]
'you shall bring' (Lev. 23.17), לֹא רֻאּוּ [loː ruːʔuː] 'they were not seen' (Job
33.21). In these cases the *dagesh* does not indicate gemination of *'aleph* but
rather signals its consonantal value, like the *mappiq* in *he*, to ensure that it is
not elided intervocalically.

Bet

Bet with *dagesh* (בּ): voiced bilabial stop [b];
Bet without *dagesh* (ב): voiced labio-dental fricative [v].

Gimel

Gimel with *dagesh* (גּ): voiced velar stop [g];

---

[68] For this feature of *dagesh* see Eldar (1984a, 27–28); Misha'el ben 'Uzzi'el,
Kitāb al-Khilaf (ed. Lipshütz 1965, 4, 18); *Sepher Taʿāme ha-Miqra* (a Hebrew adaptation of the *Hidāyat al-Qāriʾ*) ed. J. Mercerus, Paris, 1565 (facsimile edition
1978, AIIb). See further Dotan (1967, I, 15–16); Yeivin (1968, 144–145); Ben
David (1957, 401–402).

Gimel without *dagesh* (גֿ): voiced uvular fricative [ʁ].

Hidāyat al-Qāriʾ indicates that the fricative *gimel* was articulated further back than the stop (ed. Eldar 1980b, fols 10a–10b, lines 61–73). In the Karaite transcriptions fricative *gimel* is transcribed by Arabic *ghayn*, which was pronounced as a uvular fricative in the Middle Ages according to the descriptions of the Arabic grammarians (Roman 1983, 218).

Dalet

Dalet with *dagesh* (דּ): voiced post-dental stop [d];
Dalet without *dagesh* (ד): voiced post-dental fricative [ð].

The medieval scholar Isaac Israeli (ninth–tenth centuries C.E.), who had an expert knowledge of the Tiberian reading tradition, is said to have pronounced fricative *dalet* with a secondary 'emphatic' articulation (i.e. with retraction of the tongue root and increased muscular pressure) in two words, viz. אַפַּדְנוֹ 'his palace' (Dan. 11.45) and וַיְדְרְכוּ 'and they have bent' (Jer. 9.2) (Schreiner 1886, 221; Mann 1972, 670, n.106; Dukes 1845, 9, 73; Grossberg 1902, 24).

He (ה) /h/:

Glottal fricative [h].

A dot in a final *he* indicates that the letter was to be pronounced as a consonant and was not merely a *mater lectionis* for a final vowel, e.g. לָהּ [lɔːh] 'to her', but מַלְכָּה [malkɔː] 'queen'. This dot was known as *mappiq* (or in some medieval sources *mappeq*), meaning literally 'bringing out, pronouncing'. Consonantal *he* could not be pronounced with different degrees of muscular pressure and so does not occur with *dagesh* expressing gemination.

Waw (ו) /w/:

Labio-dental [v] and labio-velar semi-vowel [w].

The default pronunciation of *waw* was a labio-dental. This is indicated in a variety of medieval sources, e.g. David ben Abraham al-Fāsī, *Kitāb Jāmiʿ al-ʾAlfāẓ* (ed. Skoss 1936–1945, vol. 2, 451–452), Mishaʾel ben ʿUzziʾel, *Kitāb al-Khilaf* (ed. Lipshütz 1965, ב). Its pronunciation as [w] was restricted to contexts where it was preceded or followed by a *u* vowel, e.g. וּפֻוָּה [ufuwˈwɔː] 'and Puwwa (proper name)' (Gen. 46.13). In some manuscripts a *waw* before a *u* vowel is written with a dot as if it were the vowel *shureq*, which reflects its pronunciation as [w] rather than [v], e.g. טָווּ [tɔːˈwuː] 'they span' (Exod. 35.26) (Yeivin 1980, 285–286).

Zayin (ז) /z/

Voiced alveolar sibilant [z].

Hidāyat al-Qāriʾ mentions a variant of the letter *zayin* that the Tiberian scholars refer to as *zāy makrūkh* (Eldar 1984a, 32).[69] The term *makrūkh* was used to refer to an emphatic form of *resh* (Khan 1995). It appears, therefore, that *zayin* had an emphatic allophone [ẓ], though its distribution is unknown.

Ḥet (ח) /ḥ/

Unvoiced pharyngal fricative [ḥ].

Hidāyat al-Qāriʾ does not distinguish between the place of articulation of the laryngals and that of the pharyngals. Some medieval grammarians, however, state that *ḥet* and its voiced counterpart *ʿayin* were articulated less deep in

---

[69] The Yemenite orthoepic treatise known as the Hebrew *Maḥberet ha-Tījān*, which was based on the long version of the *Hidāya*, contains a similar statement: וכן יש להם זי"ן נקרא מכרוך ואינו ידוע אצלינו 'They (i.e. the Jews of Palestine) have a *zayin* called *makrūkh*, but it is unfamiliar to us (i.e. the Jews of Yemen)' (ed. Derenbourg 1871, 81); cf. Morag (1960, 210, n. 45)

the throat that ʾaleph and he.[70] Ḥet could not be made 'heavy' with dagesh,[71] i.e. it could not be pronounced with different degrees of muscular pressure. It is transcribed by Arabic ḥāʾ (unvoiced pharyngal fricative) in the Karaite transcriptions.

Ṭet (ט) /ṭ/:

Emphatic (retracted tongue root and increased muscular pressure) unvoiced alveolar plosive [ṭ].

According to Hidāyat al-Qāriʾ, it was articulated with the tongue tip and the gums.[72]

Yod (י) /y/

Palatal unrounded semi-vowel [j].

Saadya states that the Tiberians pronounced yod with dagesh like Arabic jīm (Commentary on the Sepher Yeṣira, ed. Lambert 1891, 42–43). According to the early Arabic grammarians, jīm was realized as a voiced palatal stop [ɟ], which had the same place of articulation as the semi-vowel [j], so presumably Saadya is referring to the realization of yod with dagesh as [ɟ], e.g. וַיְשַׁמֵּד [vajjaš'me:ð] 'and he destroyed' (1 Kings 16.12).

Kaph:

Kaph with dagesh (כּ): unvoiced aspirated velar stop [kʰ];
Kaph without dagesh (כ): unvoiced uvular fricative [χ].

Evidence for the articulation of fricative kaph further back than plosive kaph is found in Hidāyat al-Qāriʾ (Eldar 1980b, fol. 10a, lines 58–59). In the

---

[70] Ibn Janāḥ, Kitāb al-Lumaʿ (ed. Derenbourg 1886, 26–27), Menaḥem ben Saruq, Maḥberet (ed. Filipowski 1854, 6).

[71] Hidāyat al-Qāriʾ (ed. Eldar 1980b, fols 9a–9b).

[72] Hidāyat al-Qāriʾ (ed. Eldar 1980b, fol. 10b, lines 67–69).

Karaite transcriptions fricative *kaph* is represented by Arabic *khāʾ*, which was pronounced as an unvoiced uvular fricative (Roman 1983, 218). We know from Greek transcriptions that in the first half of the first millennium C.E. plosive *kaph* was aspirated (Kutscher 1965, 24–35). This was almost certainly the case also in the Tiberian pronunciation tradition in most phonetic contexts. In the Karaite transcriptions plosive *kaph* with *dagesh* is represented by Arabic *kāf*, which was aspirated (Roman 1983, 55).

Lamed (ל) /l/:

Voiced alveolar lateral continuant [l].

According to *Hidāyat al-Qāriʾ*, the articulation of this letter involved the contact of the tongue tip with the gums (Eldar 1980b, fol. 10b, lines 67–69).

Mem (מ) /m/:

Voiced bi-labial nasal [m].

Nun (נ) /n/:

Voiced alveolar nasal [n].

According to *Hidāyat al-Qāriʾ*, it was articulated with the end of the tongue and the gums (Eldar 1980b, fol. 10b, lines 67–68).

Samekh (ס) /s/:

Unvoiced alveolar sibilant [s].

ʿAyin (ע) /ʿ/:

Voiced pharyngal fricative [ʕ].

The letter could not be pronounced with different degrees of muscular pressure and so does not occur with *dagesh* expressing gemination.

Pe:

Pe with *dagesh* (פּ): unvoiced aspirated bi-labial stop [pʰ];
Pe without *dagesh* (פ): unvoiced labio-dental fricative [f].

Saadya refers to the existence of a 'hard' *pe* in the word אַפַּדְנוֹ 'his palace' (Dan. 11.45), which he describes as 'between *bet* and *pe* with *dagesh*'.[73] This appears to be referring to an unaspirated, fortis realization of [p]. One may infer from this that the normal unvoiced stop *pe* was aspirated. We know from Greek transcriptions that in the first half of the first millennium C.E. plosive *pe* was aspirated (Kutscher 1965, 24–35). We learn from one medieval source that Isaac Israeli pronounced the *dalet* in this word as emphatic (Schreiner 1886, 221; Grossberg 1902, 24). This implies that the 'hard' *pe* was also emphatic, the *dalet* being pronounced emphatic by assimilation (Steiner 1993).

Ṣade (צ) /ṣ/:

Unvoiced emphatic alveolar sibilant [ṣ].

Ibn Khaldūn refers to a voiced allophone of *ṣade* [ẓ] in the pronunciation of the name אֲמַצְיָהוּ, i.e. [ʔamaẓˈjɔːhuː] (Schreiner 1886, 254).

Qoph (ק) /q/:

Unvoiced uvular or post-velar unaspirated plosive [q].

According to *Hidāyat al-Qāriʾ*, *qoph* was articulated with the 'middle of the tongue', and so further forward than fricative *gimel* and *kaph*, which were pronounced with the 'back third of the tongue' (ed. Eldar 1980b, fols 10a–10b, lines 61–72). This suggests a post-velar point of articulation. In the Karaite transcriptions this letter is represented by Arabic *qāf*, which, according to the medieval Arabic grammarians, was unaspirated and articulated between the velar stop *kāf* and the uvular fricatives *khāʾ* and *ghayn* (Roman

---

[73] Commentary on the *Sepher Yeṣira* (ed. Lambert 1891, 42).

1983, 110). In the Greek transcriptions from the first half of the first millennium C.E. *qoph* is represented by *kappa*, which was an unaspirated [k].

Resh (ר) /r/:

(i) Voiced uvular roll [ʀ] or uvular frictionless continuant [ʁ] and (ii) emphatic apico-alveolar roll [r̠].

According to *Hidāyat al-Qāriʾ*, the Tiberians pronounced *resh* in two different ways, as was the case with the letters בגדכפת *bgdkpt*. Its basic articulation was with 'the middle third of the tongue', as was the case with *qoph* and plosive *kaph*, suggesting an advanced uvular position. It is not made clear whether it was a roll [ʀ] or frictionless continuant [ʁ]. The secondary form of *resh* was pronounced in the environment of the alveolar consonants דזצתטסלן *dzṣttsln*. It was alveolar, by partial assimilation to these consonants, and pronounced emphatic (retracted tongue root) with slight retroflexion of the tongue tip (referred to in the sources as *makrūkh*).[74] According to the medieval sources this apico-alveolar emphatic *resh* occurred when preceded by the consonants דזצתטסלן or followed by לן and when either *resh* or one of these consonants has *shewa*. This can be reformulated as the rule that alveolar *resh* occurs when in immediate contact with a preceding alveolar, e.g., בְּמַזְרֶה [bamizˈr̠ɛː] 'with a pitch fork' (Jer. 15.7), מַצְרֵף [maṣˈr̠eːf] 'crucible' (Prov. 17.3), or in the same syllable as a preceding alveolar, e.g., דַּרְכּוֹ [darˈkoː] 'his way' (Gen. 24.21), טַרְפֵּי [ṭarpeː] 'the leaves of' (Ezek. 17.9), a consonant with vocalic *shewa* being treated as belonging to the same syllable as the following consonant (§10.5), e.g., צְרוּפָה [ṣar̠uːˈfɔː] 'refined (fs)' (2 Sam. 22.31), or when the *resh* is in immediate contact with or in the same syllable as a following ל or ן, e.g., עַרְלֵי־לֵב [ʕar̠leː-leːv] 'uncircumcised in heart' (Jer. 9.25), גָּרְנִי [gɔr̠niː] 'my threshing-floor' (Isa. 21.10), רַנְּנוּ [r̠annaˈnuː] 'rejoice (mpl)!' (Ps. 33.1), רְנָנָה [r̠anɔːˈnɔː] 'joyful cry' (Job 3.7). Elsewhere *resh* had a uvular realization, e.g., רֶכֶב [ˈʀɛːxɛv] 'chariotry' (Exod.

---

[74] The evidence for this is presented in Khan (1995). See also Khan (2013a).

14.9), מַרְאֶה [maʀˈʔɛː] 'appearance' (Gen. 12.11), שָׁמַר [ʃɔːˈmaːʀ] 'he kept' (Gen. 37.11), אֶרְדּוֹף [ʔɛʀˈdoːf] 'I pursue' (Ps. 18.38).

Sin (שׂ) /s/:

Unvoiced alveolar sibilant [s].

This had the same pronunciation as *samekh*.

Shin (שׁ) /š/:

Unvoiced palato-alveolar fricative [ʃ].

Taw:

Taw with *dagesh* (תּ): unvoiced aspirated alveolar stop [tʰ];
Taw without *dagesh* (ת): unvoiced alveolar fricative [θ].

According to *Hidāyat al-Qāri*ʾ, *taw* was articulated with 'the end of the tongue and the flesh of the teeth', i.e. the gums or alveolar ridge (ed. Eldar 1980b, fol. 10b, lines 67–69). Likewise Saadya describes the place of articulation of *taw* as being adjacent to the inside of the upper teeth.[75] When the letter had *dagesh*, the tongue was pressed firmly against the gums. When it was without *dagesh*, the tongue was pressed lightly against the gums. Both forms of the letter were articulated in the same place according to the medieval sources.

We know from Greek transcriptions that in the first half of the first millennium C.E. plosive *taw* was pronounced with aspiration (Kutscher 1965, 24–35). This was presumably the case also in the Tiberian pronunciation tradition. In the Karaite transcriptions plosive *taw* with *dagesh* is represented by Arabic *tā*ʾ, which was aspirated according to the medieval Arabic grammarians (Roman 1983, 55).

---

[75] Commentary on *Sepher Yeṣira* (ed. Lambert 1891, 75).

10.2. Distribution of the Variants of the Letters בגדכפת

In general, the fricative variants of these letters (i.e. the forms written without a *dagesh* sign: [v], [ʁ], [ð], [χ], [f] and [θ], respectively) occur after a vowel when the letter is not geminated, e.g. רַב [ˈʁaːv] 'much' (Gen. 24.25), יִשְׁכְּבוּ [jiškaˈvuː] 'they will lie' (Isa. 43.17). In principle, therefore, the stop and fricative variants appear to be allophones conditioned by the environment. In many cases, however, the preceding vowel had been elided in some previous stage of the language but the consonant nevertheless remained a fricative, e.g. בְּכָתְבוֹ [baχɔθˈvoː] 'when he had written' (Jer. 45.1) < *bakutubō*, מַלְכֵי [malˈχeː] 'kings of' (Gen. 17.16) < *malakē*. In a few such cases a plosive and a fricative are in free variation, e.g. רִשְׁפֵּי [ʁišˈfeː] (Ps. 76.4), רִשְׁפֵּי [ʁišˈpʰeː] (Cant. 8.6) 'flames'. The distribution of the plosive and fricative allophones, therefore, is not completely predicable from the phonetic context in Tiberian Hebrew. Consequently the plosive and fricative variants of the letters should be distinguished in a synchronic phonological representation, e.g. מַלְכֵי /malχē/ [malˈχeː] 'kings of' (Gen. 17.16), בִּנְפֹּל /binfōl/ [binˈfoːl] 'at the falling of' (Isa. 30.25). In the corpus of the Hebrew Bible, however, there is no certain minimal pair arising from the phonemicization of the variants of the *bgdkpt* consonants, though such oppositions could hypothetically occur in Tiberian Hebrew. Such minimal pairs are found in Aramaic, where the *bgdkpt* consonants were likewise phonemicized (Khan 2005, 84–87).

When a *bgdkpt* consonant occurs at the beginning of a word and the preceding word ends in a vowel, the general rule is that the consonant is fricative if the accent of the preceding word is conjunctive or if the preceding word is connected by *maqqeph* but is plosive if the accent of the preceding word is disjunctive, e.g. שְׁלֹשָׁה בָנִים 'three sons' (Gen. 6.10) but זָכָר וּנְקֵבָה בָּרָאָם 'male and female he created them' (Gen. 5.2). There are several exceptions to this rule, one being the construction known as *deḥiq*, which is discussed below.

10.3. Vowel Signs

The basic vowel signs of the Tiberian vocalization represent qualitative distinctions.

Pataḥ (◌):

Open, unrounded front [a].

Seghol (◌):

Front, half-open unrounded [ɛ].

Qameṣ (◌):

Back, half-open rounded [ɔ].

Ṣere (◌):

Front, half-close unrounded [e].

Ḥolem (◌):.

Back, half-close rounded [o].

Ḥireq (◌):

Front, close, unrounded [i].

Shureq (ו), *Qibbuṣ* (◌):

Back, close, rounded [u].

10.4. Vowel Length

The length of vowels represented by the vowel signs are predictable from syllable structure and the placement of stress. Vowels are pronounced long when they are either (i) in a stressed syllable or (ii) in an open unstressed syllable. Elsewhere the vowel is pronounced short. Examples: מֶלֶךְ [ˈmɛːlɛχ] 'king', יִשְׁמַע [jiʃˈmaːʕ] 'he hears', חָכְמָה [ḥɔχˈmɔː] 'wisdom', הַהוּא [haːˈhuː] 'that', מִחוּץ [miːˈḥuːṣ] 'outside'. In the orthography short [u] is predominantly represented by *qibbuṣ*, e.g. יֻקַּם [yuqˈqaːm] 'he will be avenged', but is occasionally represented by *shureq*, e.g. יוּשַּׁד [juʃˈʃaːð] 'it will be destroyed' (Hos. 10.14). The vowels *ḥolem* and *ṣere* are invariably long and have no short variants. This also is essentially dependent on stress and syllable struc-

ture, in that they occur only in the aforementioned environments that condition vowel length, e.g. כּוֹהֵן [koːˈheːn] 'priest', הֵקִים [heːˈqiːm] 'he raised', יָקוֹם
[jɔːˈqoːm] 'may he rise'.

Many words carry a secondary stress in addition to the main stress, e.g.
הָאָדָם [ˌhɔːʔɔːˈ ðɔːm] 'the man' (Gen. 2.19), נִתְחַכְּמָה [ˌniːθħakkaˈmɔː] 'let us
deal wisely' (Exod. 1.10).

As has been remarked, a vowel in an unstressed closed syllable was, in
principle, short. If, however, it was followed by a series of contiguous consonants of relatively weak articulation (e.g. אהעחינל ʾhʿhynl), then the vowel
was sometimes lengthened, even when not stressed. This occurred in certain
prefixes of the verbs היה hyh 'be' and חיה ḥyh 'live', namely the ḥireq of prefixes before he or ḥet, e.g. יִהְיֶה [jiːhˈjɛː] 'he will be', and the pataḥ of the conjunctive prefix ו wa- before yod, e.g. וַיְהִי [vaːjˈhiː] 'and it was' (Khan 1994a).
Such lengthening is occasionally found elsewhere and is marked by the
gaʿya sign, e.g. הֲשָׁמַע עָם [haˈʃɔːmaːʕ ˈʕɔːm] 'did any people hear?' (Deut.
4.33), שְׁמַע־נָא [ʃamaːʕ-ˈnɔː] 'listen' (1 Sam. 28.22), וּפְתַחְיָה [ufθaːħˈjɔː] 'and
Pethahiah' (Neh. 11.24).[76] The intention of the lengthening of the unstressed
vowel in such contexts was, it seems, to ensure that adjacent weak letters
were not elided in the reading.

The duration of long vowels varied considerably. From the medieval
sources we are able to infer the existence of several different degrees in the
relative duration of long vowels. Most of these were conditioned by differences in stress, vowel height or consonant strength. We shall mention here
some of the known cases of differences in relative duration of long vowels:[77]

1. Stressed long vowels were longer than unstressed long vowels, e.g.
in the word הַהוּא [haːˈhuː] 'that' the [uː] was longer than the [aː].[78]

---

[76] For this type of gaʿya see Yeivin (1980, 262).

[77] For these variations see Khan (1987; 1989; 1994; 1996a)

[78] This may explain forms such as הֶחָדַלְתִּי (Jud. 9.9) 'Have I ceased?' in
which a pretonic long vowel has been reduced to a ḥateph vowel.

2. A long vowel with secondary stress was longer than a long vowel in an unstressed syllable, e.g. in the word הָאָדָם [ˌhɔːʔɔːˈðɔːm] 'the man' (Gen. 2.19) the second [ɔː] was longer than the other two.

3. Long vowels in open syllables that took secondary stress marked by major *gaʿya*, e.g. הָאָדָם [ˌhɔːʔɔːˈðɔːm] 'man' (Gen. 1.27), were of greater duration than vowels in closed syllables lengthened by secondary stress marked by minor *gaʿya* e.g. נִתְחַכְּמָה [ˌniːθħakkaˈmɔː] 'let us deal wisely' (Exod. 1.10). This difference in duration is reflected in the medieval terminology: *gaʿya gedola* ('major *gaʿya*') vs. *gaʿya qeṭanna* ('minor *gaʿya*') (Khan 1992c).

4. A high vowel [iː, uː] in a closed syllable with secondary stress marked by minor *gaʿya* was shorter than a low vowel [aː] in the same conditions, e.g. in the words נִתְחַכְּמָה [ˌniːθħakkaˈmɔː] 'let us deal wisely' (Exod. 1.10) and וַתִּצְפְּנֵהוּ [vaːttiṣpaˈneːhuː] 'and she hid him' (Exod. 2.2), the [iː] vowel of the first was shorter than the [aː] vowel of the second.

5. The high vowel [iː] of prefixes of the verbs היה and חיה was shorter than the low vowel [aː] in prefixes of these verbs, e.g in the forms יִהְיֶה [jiːhˈjɛː] 'he will be' and וַיְהִי [vaːjˈhiː] 'and it was', the [iː] of the first was shorter than the [aː] of the second.

6. The high vowel [iː] of the prefixes of the verbs היה and חיה was shorter than [iː] in a stressed syllable or an unstressed open syllable but longer than [iː] in a closed syllable with secondary stress marked by minor *gaʿya*, e.g. in the words אִם [ˈʔiːm] 'if', יִהְיֶה [jiːhˈjɛː] 'he will be' and נִתְחַכְּמָה [ˌniːθħakkaˈmɔː] 'let us deal wisely' (Exod. 1.10), the three [iː] vowels were of decreasing degrees of length.

7. The [aː] vowel in prefixes of the verbs היה and חיה (e.g. וַיְהִי [vaːjˈhiː]) and other words before two weak consonants (e.g. הֲשָׁמַע עָם [haˈʃɔːmaːʕ ˈʕɔːm] 'did any people hear?' Deut. 4.33) was longer than an [aː] vowel in a closed syllable with secondary stress marked by minor *gaʿya* (e.g. וַתִּצְפְּנֵהוּ [vaːttiṣpaˈneːhuː] 'and she hid him' Exod. 2.2).

A final unstressed long vowel underwent particular reduction in duration in the construction known as *deḥiq*, i.e. where *dagesh* occurs on the initial letter of a word when the preceding word ends in a long vowel and has a conjunctive accent on the penultimate syllable.[79] *Hidāyat al-Qāriʾ* describes the phenomenon of *deḥiq* as the 'compression' of the final vowel: 'The vowel that follows the accent in בָּ֫ם וְאָעִידָה (Deut. 31.28) is not extended but is considerably compressed'.[80] According to this source the compression takes place also in short words that are connected by *maqqeph* to a following word when the initial consonant of the second word has *dagesh*: 'The compression may take place in a word without an accent if it is a short word as in מַה־תֹּאמַר (1 Sam. 20.4), זֶה־בְּנִי (1 Kings 3.23), מַה־בָּרִי (Prov. 31.2), וּמֶה־תַּעֲשֶׂה (Josh. 7.9) and the like.' This implies that the *pataḥ* in the word מַה־ before *dagesh* was long, though of decreased duration. The pronunciation of the *pataḥ* as a long vowel is confirmed by the Karaite transcriptions into Arabic script, which represent it by the *mater lectionis ʾalif*, e.g. מַה־תִּתֶּן־לִי) ما تتن لى Gen. 15.2).[81]

10.5. Syllable Structure and Shewa

In addition to the basic vowel signs, the Tiberian vocalization system employs the *shewa* sign (ְ) to mark either a short vowel or zero, e.g. יִשְׁמְרוּ [jiʃmaˈʀuː] 'they guard'. As can be seen in the phonetic transcription, the vocalic *shewa* was normally pronounced as a short vowel with the quality of *pataḥ* [a]. We know from a variety of sources that this was in principle no shorter than a *pataḥ* in a closed unstressed syllable.[82] In some contexts, however, it was realized with a different quality due to the influence of the phonetic environment. This was so when *shewa* preceded a guttural consonant or *yod*. Before a guttural it was realized as a short vowel with the quality of the vowel on the guttural, e.g. בְּאֵר [beˈʔeːʀ] 'well', מְאֹד [moˈʔoːð] 'very'. Before *yod* it was realized as a short vowel with the quality of short *ḥireq* [i], e.g. בְּיוֹם [biˈjoːm] 'on the day'. From Masoretic sources and Judaeo-Arabic

---

[79] For the conditions in which *deḥiq* is found in the Tiberian Masoretic Bible see Yeivin (1980, 289–292).

[80] Eldar (1984b, ו).

[81] See Khan (1989; 1996a) for further details.

[82] The evidence is presented in detail in Khan (1987, 37–39). See also Khan (2013b).

texts with Tiberian vocalization we know that vocalic *shewa* was equivalent in length to short vowels in unstressed closed syllables (Khan 1987, 37–39; Khan 1992b). According to the Masoretic sources, however, a consonant with a vocalic *shewa* did not constitute a syllable. Rather such a *shewa* was said to bind one consonant to the next in order to form a syllable (the sources use the Arabic term *maqṭaᶜ*) (Levy 1936, אff; Eldar 1978, 185–187). A word such as יִשְׁמְרוּ was analysed in these sources as consisting of two syllables [jiʃ.maʀuː]. The short [a], which was the realization of the *shewa*, was an epenthetic vowel breaking the cluster at the onset of a syllable. From a synchronic point of view, therefore, at some underlying level it was zero. It was for this reason that both phonetic zero (silent *shewa*) and an epenthetic vowel breaking a cluster (vocalic *shewa*) were represented by the *shewa* sign, which was intended to mark zero. Vocalic *shewa*, therefore, should be interpreted as an allophone of zero.[83] The non-syllabic nature of vocalic *shewa* is reflected by some features of Tiberian phonology. One clear example is the alternation pattern of the allophones of Tiberian *resh*. The apico-alveolar allophone [ɾ] occurred when (i) it was preceded by one of the alveolar consonants דזטסצתלן or was followed by לן and (ii) when the *resh* or one of these alveolar letters had *shewa* or when *resh* occurred at the end of the word: דַּרְכְּמוֹנִים [daɾkamoːˈniːm] 'drachmas' (Ezra 2.69), בְּמִזְרֶה [bamizˈɾɛː] 'with a pitch fork' (Jer. 15.7), צְרוּפָה [ṣaɾuːˈfɔː] 'refined' (2 Sam. 22.31). When an alveolar preceding a *resh* was vocalized with a vowel sign, the *resh* was realized with its uvular allophone [ʀ], e.g. תָּרוּץ [tɔːˈʀuːṣ] 'you run' (Prov. 4.12). In the three forms דַּרְכְּמוֹנִים [daɾkamoːˈniːm], צְרוּפָה [ṣaɾuːˈfɔː] and תָּרוּץ [tɔːˈʀuːṣ] the *resh* is separated from a preceding alveolar by a vowel, but the [ɾ] allophone only occurs in the first two. The most obvious explanation is that only in the first two does the *resh* occur in the same syllable as the alveolar, so the syllabic divisions would be [daɾ.kamoː.ˈniːm], [ṣaɾuː.ˈfɔː] and [tɔː.ˈʀuːṣ].

The main principles for the distribution of vocalic and silent *shewa* are as follows. The *shewa* was read as vocalic at the beginning of a word. The

---

[83] For further details regarding to the analysis of syllable structure see Khan (2013c).

only exception was the *shewa* in forms of the feminine numeral שְׁתַּיִם 'two', which was silent ['ʃtaːyim]. According to some sources this word was pronounced by the Tiberian Masoretes with a prosthetic vowel: אֶשְׁתַּיִם [ʔɛʃ'taːjim].[84] At the end of a word *shewa* was silent. When two *shewas* occur together at the end of a word, most sources state that both were silent, e.g. וַיֵּבְךְ [vaj'jeːvk] 'and he wept' (Gen. 45.15). According to some sources, however, the second *shewa* was vocalic, unless the word occurred in major pause, in which case all sources agree that both were silent, e.g. וַיֵּבְךְ [vaj'jeːvk] 'and he wept' (Gen. 29.11).[85] Within a word, when two *shewas* occur on successive letters, the first was silent and the second vocalic, e.g. יִשְׁמְרוּ [jiʃma'ʀuː] 'they will keep' (2 Chron. 23.6). A *shewa* under a geminated letter with *dagesh* was vocalic. Elsewhere a *shewa* within a word was generally silent, e.g. שֹׁמְרִים [ˌʃoːm'ʀiːm] 'guarding' (Num. 3.38), אָכְלָה [ʔɔːχ'lɔː] 'it (fs.) devoured' (2 Sam. 18.8). The Masoretic sources list a number of exceptions to this rule. One notable case is a *shewa* under the first of a pair of identical consonants, which was vocalic if the preceding vowel was long, e.g. לָקְקוּ [lɔːqa'quː] 'they licked' (1 Kings 21.19). If the preceding vowel was short, however, the *shewa* was silent, e.g. הִנְנִי [hin'niː] 'behold me' (Gen. 6.17).[86] In six words, however, *shewa* on the second of two identical letters after a long vowel is silent, in all of which the long vowel has the main stress, e.g., יְמְצָאֻנְנִי [jimsɔːʔuːnni] 'they (m) will find me' (Prov. 8.17) (*Diqduqe ha-Ṭeʿamim*, ed. Dotan 1967, §5).

According to Ben Asher's *Diqduqe ha-Ṭeʿamim* and other Masoretic sources, if *resh* with *shewa* is the first letter of a noun and is preceded by an affix that has *qameṣ* or *ṣere*, the *shewa* is pronounced vocal, e.g., הָרְוָחָה [hɔːʀavɔː'hɔː] 'the relief' (Exod. 8.11), מֵרְפִידִים [meːʀafiː'ðiːm] 'from Rephidim' (Exod. 19.2). Elsewhere when *resh* with *shewa* is preceded by a long vowel, however, the *shewa* is generally silent, as is the usual rule in the Tiberian tradition, e.g., in the verbal forms יָרְדוּ [jɔːʀ'ðuː] 'they went down'

---

[84] See Levy (1936, 31–33) for the sources.

[85] See Khan (1996b, 16) for the sources.

[86] For further exceptional cases see Yeivin (1980, 275–282).

(Exod. 15.5), יֵרְדוּ [jeːʁˈðuː] 'they (m) will come down' (1 Sam. 13.12), יֹרְדִים [joːʁˈðiːm] 'coming down (mpl)' (Jud. 9.37).

A *shewa* on the medial radical of the verbal roots גר"ש 'drive out', אכ"ל 'to eat', בר"ד 'bless', יר"ד 'to go down', and הל"ך 'to go' is vocalic after a long vowel in certain circumstances, according to Ben Asher. In forms from the root גר"ש it is vocalic when the third radical has *seghol*, e.g., אֲגָרְשֶׁנּוּ [ʔaʁɔːʁaˈʃɛnnuː] 'I will drive them out' (Exod. 23.30), but is otherwise silent, e.g., וַיְגָרְשׁוּ [wajʁɔːʁaˈʃuː] 'and they drove out' (Jud. 11.2). The same applies to the root אכ"ל. So the *shewa* is vocalic in, for example, תֹּאכֲלֶנָּה [toːχaˈlɛːnnuː] 'you (ms) shall eat it' (Ezek. 4.12), but silent in תֹאכְלוּן [toːχˈluːn] 'you (mpl) shall [not] eat' (Num. 11.19), the only exception being אֹכְלֶיהָ [ʔoːχˈlɛːhɔː] 'those (m) who eat it' (Ecc. 5.10), in which it is silent. In forms with *shewa* on the *resh* from the root בר"ד 'bless', if the accent is on the *bet*, the *shewa* is silent, e.g., וְהִתְבָּרְכוּ בוֹ [wihiθˈbɔːʁχuː ˈvoː] 'they will bless themselves in him' (Jer. 4.2), but if the accent is on the *kaf*, the *shewa* is vocalic, e.g., בָּרֲכֵנִי [bɔːʁaˈχeːniː] 'bless (ms) me!' (Gen. 27.34). When forms from the roots יר"ד 'to come down' and הל"ך 'to go' are followed by נָא with *dagesh* due to the rule of *deḥiq*, then a *shewa* on the medial radical is vocalic, e.g., אֵרֲדָה־נָּא [ʔeːʁaðɔː-nˈnɔː] 'I will go down' (Gen. 18.21), אֵלֲכָה נָּא [ʔeːlaχɔː- nnɔː] 'let me go' (Exod. 4.18), but otherwise is silent. Saadya gives the general rule that *shewa* after a long vowel is always vocalic when the vowel two syllables after it is stressed and is preceded by *dagesh*,[87] so it is vocalic also in forms such as נוֹתְרָה־בָּהּ [noːθarɔː-ˈbbɔː] 'there is left in it' (Ezek. 14.22).

As remarked, a *shewa* in the middle of a word after a short vowel is silent, e.g., יִתְרוֹ [jiθˌʁoː] 'Jethro'. If the short vowel is lengthened by what Yeivin calls a 'phonetic *gaʿya*',[88] then the *shewa* is vocalic. This applies to a *shewa* on *mem* after the definite article with *pataḥ*, e.g., הַמְנַדִּים [haːmanadˈdiːm] 'the ones who drive away' (Amos 6.3), and also elsewhere, e.g., בַּנְחֻשְׁתַּיִם [baːnaħuʃˈtaːjim] 'with bronze fetters' (Jud. 16.21), וּשְׁלַח [ˌuːʃaˈlaːħ] 'and send (ms)' (2 Kings 9.17), הֲתִמְלֹךְ [haθiːmaˈloːχ] 'are you a king?' (Jer. 22.15). When a short vowel has a musical *gaʿya*, known as 'mi-

---

[87] Dotan (1997, 464–466).

[88] Yeivin (1980, 257–264).

nor *gaʿya'*, the following *shewa* is silent. Minor *gaʿyot* occur predominantly on words with disjunctive accents on a closed syllable that is separated from the stress syllable by another syllable followed by vocal *shewa* or a *ḥaṭef*, e.g., נִתְחַכְּמָה [ˌniːθḥakkaˈmɔː] 'let us deal wisely' (Exod. 1.10), מִשְׁתַּחֲוִים [ˌmiːʃtaːḥaˈviːm] 'prostrating (mpl) themselves' (Gen. 37.9).[89] A word such as הַמְשַׂחֲקוֹת 'the ones (fpl) playing' (1 Sam. 18.7), therefore, has a structure suitable for minor *gaʿya* and so it is read with minor *gaʿya* and the *shewa* after the *pataḥ* is silent [ˌhaːmśaːḥaˈqoːθ].[90]

There was some variation in the reading of *shewa* among the Tiberian Masoretes, notably between Ben Asher and Ben Naphtali. The readings with vocalic *shewa* after long vowels given above are those of Ben Asher. Ben Naphtali read the *shewa* as silent in some cases.[91] Some manuscripts, moreover, mark a *ḥaṭef pataḥ* to represent vocalic *shewa* after long vowels in words that are not mentioned in Masoretic treatises, e.g., Aleppo codex אָזְלַת [ˈʔɔːzalaθ] (St. Petersburg codex אָזְלַת) '[their power] has gone' (Deut. 32.36).

The reading of a *shewa* as vocalic rather than silent in the Tiberian tradition was to some extent independent of rules relating to phonetic environment. It was sometimes read as vocalic in morphological patterns where it would normally be silent, e.g., אִמְרוֹת [ʔiːmaˈroːθ] 'the words of' (Ps. 12.7), הֲתִמְלֹךְ [haθiːmaˈloːχ] 'are you a king?' (Jer. 22.15). In these cases the vowel is lengthened before vocalic *shewa*. Sometimes the preceding consonant is geminated, e.g., מִקְּדָשׁ [miqqaˈðɔːʃ] 'sanctuary' (Exod. 15.17), עִקְּבוֹת [ʕiqqaˈvoːθ] 'footprints of' (Ps. 89.52), מַמְּרֹרִים [mammaʀoːˈʀiːm] 'bitterness' (Job 9.18). In יְרַדְּף [jiːˌraddoːf] 'let him pursue' (Ps. 7.6) the consonant after the vocalic *shewa* is geminated and so the letter is vocalized with a *pataḥ* sign. The elongation of such words by reading a silent *shewa* as vocalic sometimes seems to have a pragmatic purpose, to give the word more discourse prominence.

---

[89] Yeivin (1980, 244–245).

[90] Yeivin (1980:278–279).

[91] Cf. *Kitāb al-Khilaf* (ed. Lipschütz 1965, 17).

The *shewa* sign is combined with the vowels *pataḥ*, *seghol* and *qameṣ* to form the so-called *ḥateph* vowels (◌ֲ, ◌ֱ, ◌ֳ). The *ḥateph* signs were marked mainly under the guttural letters, where the pronunciation of the *shewa* was less predictable than under other letters. For instance, there were variations between silent and vocalic *shewa* in verbal forms such as וַיַּחְבְּשׁוּ [vajjaḥba'ʃuː] 'and they saddled' (1 Kings 13.13) versus וַיַּחֲבֹשׁ [ˌvaːjjaːħaˈvoːʃ] 'and he saddled' (Gen. 22.3). In these cases the *ḥateph* sign represents an epenthetic vowel and can be regarded as equivalent to vocalic *shewa*. The *shewa* was explicitly marked as vocalic by the addition of a vowel sign due to the fact that the Masoretes considered that readers would have had greater difficulty predicting its realization than the realization of *shewa* in other contexts. Recent research has identified various linguistic factors that condition the distribution of the epenthetic marked by *ḥateph* vowels in the environment of gutturals (DeCaen 2003; Alvestad and Edzard 2009), but the fact remains that the occurrence of the epenthetic in the environment of gutturals was perceived to cause difficulties to readers by the Masoretes.[92] The quality of an epenthetic also deviates from the normal rules, which likewise motivated the addition of a vowel sign to the *shewa*. A *shewa* on a guttural, for example, retained the quality of [a] even if it preceded a guttural that was followed by a vowel of a different quality, e.g. יִמְחֲאוּ [jimħaʔuː] 'they clap' (Ps. 98.8). An epenthetic vowel on a guttural became assimilated to the quality of a preceding *seghol* or *qameṣ*, e.g. הֶעֱמִיד [hɛˈʕɛˈmiːð] 'he set up', הָעֳמַד [hɔˈʕɔˈmaːð] 'it was set up'.

Ḥateph signs are written under non-guttural consonants in various contexts. In some such cases the *ḥateph* is an epenthetic vowel, i.e. vocalic *shewa* that has been graphically disambiguated due to the deviation of its realization from the norm. The marking of such epenthetics by *ḥateph* signs was not fixed in the Masoretic tradition and there is considerable variation in the manuscripts. Some of the exceptional cases of vocalic *shewa* presented above have *ḥateph pataḥ* in the St. Petersburgh (Firkovitch I, B19a) codex, e.g. תֹּאכֲלֶנּוּ [toːχaˈlɛːnnuː] 'you (ms) shall eat it' (Ezek. 4.12). The marking

---

[92] The tendency for variation in the distribution of *ḥateph* vowels appears to have been exploited to express a semantic distinction between the verb יַעְקֹב 'he surplants' (Jer. 9.3) and the proper name יַעֲקֹב.

of *ḥateph pataḥ* is more frequent in the Aleppo codex, under the first of two identical consonants that is preceded by a long vowel, e.g. לְקֲקוּ [lɔːqaˈquː] 'they licked' (1 Kings 21.19).

In some cases a consonant with a *ḥateph qameṣ* or *ḥateph seghol* appears to have the status of a syllable and so the sign is marking a phonological short vowel nucleus rather than an epenthetic. This applies notably to *ḥateph qameṣ* on non-guttural consonants in words such as דֳּמִי [dɔˈmiː] 'silence', צֳרִי [ṣɔˈʀiː] 'balsam', צִפֳּרִים [ṣippʰɔˈʀiːm] 'birds', קֳדָשִׁים [qɔðɔːˈʃiːm] 'holy things'. We learn from medieval sources that the *resh* in the word צֳרִי was realized as an uvular [ṣɔˈʀiː] whereas when the *ṣade* had a *shewa*, as in צְרוּפָה, the *resh* was realized as apico-alveolar [ṣaṛuːˈfɔː]. This indicates that the *resh* in צֳרִי was separated from the *ṣade* by a syllable boundary, as in תָּרוּץ [tɔːˈʀuːṣ]. A *ḥateph qameṣ* on a non-guttural consonant is, moreover, frequently treated like a full vowel nucleus in an open syllable with regard to the placement of secondary stress. In words such as קֳדָשִׁים secondary stress may be placed on the first syllable marked by major *gaʿya*. As a result the *ḥateph qameṣ* is replaced by a *qameṣ*, reflecting its lengthening by the *gaʿya*, e.g. קָֽדָשִׁים [ˌqɔːðɔːˈʃiːm] 'holy things' (Exod. 29.37). Major *gaʿya* (referred to in the Masoretic sources as *gaʿya gedola*) was typically marked on open syllables containing a long vowel, e.g. הָֽאָדָם [ˌhɔːʔɔːˈðɔːm] 'man' (Gen. 1.27). Secondary stress was in some cases marked on a closed syllable with a short vowel by what was known as 'minor *gaʿya*' (*gaʿya qeṭanna*), resulting in the lengthening of the vowel, e.g. וַֽתִּצְפְּנֵהוּ [vaːttiṣpaˈneːhuː] 'and she hid him' (Exod. 2.2). It was even marked occasionally on a *shewa* or epenthetic *ḥateph* vowel (known as *shewa gaʿya*), as a result of which these were lengthened, e.g. תְּֽשַׁלְּחוֹ [ˌtaːʃallaˈħuː] 'you shall let go' (Jer. 34.14), עֲֽלִיּוֹתָיו [ˌʕaːlijjoːˈθɔːv] 'his chambers' (Ps. 104.3) (Khan 2009).

Major *gaʿya* can be distinguished from minor *gaʿya* and *shewa gaʿya* by their different patterns of marking in the early Masoretic manuscripts. The marking of major *gaʿya* was not standardized and there are numerous differences across the manuscripts, while the marking of minor *gaʿya* and *shewa gaʿya* was fixed and is largely uniform across the manuscripts. Unlike the major *gaʿya* on קֳדָשִׁים [ˌqɔːðɔːˈʃiːm], an epenthetic *ḥateph* sign with *gaʿya* is only rarely replaced by a full vowel sign. In sum the marking of *gaʿya* indicates that the *ḥaṭeph qameṣ* in קָדָשִׁים was treated as if it were the nucleus of an open syllable rather than an epenthetic vowel.

In a few words beginning with a guttural consonant, a *ḥaṭeph qameṣ* or *ḥaṭeph seghol* on the initial guttural appears to stand in phonemic opposition to *ḥaṭeph paṭaḥ*, e.g. חֳלִי [ħɔˈliː] 'illness' versus חֲלִי 'ornament', עֱלִי [ʕɛˈliː] 'pestle' versus עֲלִי [ʕaˈliː] 'go up! (fs.)'. The forms with *ḥaṭeph paṭaḥ* have the morphological pattern of forms such as שְׁבִי [ʃaˈviː] 'captivity' and גְּלִי [gaˈliː] 'uncover! (fs.)', respectively with *shewa*. The *ḥaṭeph paṭaḥ* in these forms, therefore, can be regarded as an epenthetic and at some underlying level the forms would be monosyllabic. The *ḥaṭeph qameṣ* and *ḥaṭeph seghol*, on the other hand, would be short syllable nuclei.

When a long vowel taking secondary stress in the form of an accent or major *gaʿya* was followed by *shewa*, the *shewa* was generally silent, e.g. שׁוֹמְרִים [ˌʃoːmˈʁiːm] 'guarding (pl.)', אָכְלָה [ˌʔɔːχˈlɔː] 'she ate'. Normally such secondary stress is separated from the main stress by a buffer syllable or at least by a vocalic *shewa*. The occurrence of secondary stress in these forms suggests that a closed syllable containing a long vowel was split by an epenthetic vowel functioning metrically as a buffer, which would have resulted phonetically in an extra-long vowel: [ˌʃoːomˈʁiːim], [ˌʔɔːɔχˈlɔ]. The most compelling evidence for the insertion of this epenthetic vowel in a closed syllable with a long vowel is the *paṭaḥ furtivum*, e.g. רוּחַ [ˈʁuːaḥ] 'spirit'. This short unstressed *a* vowel is to be interpreted as the epenthetic vowel which has shifted quality through assimilation to the vocal tract configuration of the following laryngal or pharyngal consonant.

It is a rather complex matter to establish the synchronic phonological representation of the vowels of the Tiberian reading tradition. Taking into account all the details of the foregoing description, one must distinguish between (i) vowels which are invariably long and include length in their underlying phonological representation and (ii) vowels whose length is determined by stress and syllable structure and so are of unspecified length at a phonological level.

The long vowel phonemes include: long *qameṣ* /ɔ̄/, *ḥolem* /ō/, *ṣere* /ē/, long *shureq* /ū/, long *ḥireq* /ī/ (typically written with *yod*), e.g., יָד /yɔ̄ð/ [yɔːöð] 'hand', כֹּהֵן /kōhēn/ [koːheːen] 'priest', יִירְשׁוּ /yīrˈšū/ [jiːiʁˈʃuː] 'they inherit'.

The vowel phonemes unspecified as to length include: *patah* /a/, *seghol* /ɛ/, *hireq* /i/, *qibbus/shureq* /u/. In principle these are long when they bear stress, e.g., יִשְׁמַע /jiʃˈmaʕ/ [jiʃˈmaːʕ] 'he hears', נַעַר /ˈnaʕar/ [ˈnaːʕaʀ] 'boy', כַּרְמֶל /karˈmɛl/ [kaʀˈmɛːl] 'plantation', מֶלֶךְ /ˈmɛlɛχ/ [ˈmɛːlɛχ] 'king', or syllabified with two moras in open unstressed syllables, e.g., הַהוּא /haa.hū/ [haːˈhuː] 'that' and מִחוּץ /mii.ḥūṣ/ [miːˈhuːuṣ] 'outside'.[93] In unstressed closed syllables they are short.

To the second category of vowels we should add also /e/ and /o/ without specified length. These are represented by the *sere* and *holem* vowel signs, respectively, in the stressed syllables of certain forms. Since stressed vowels are always long, on a phonetic level these are not distinguishable from cases of *sere* and *holem* that represent phonemes with underlying length. This is necessary to account for apparent discrepancies in the historical development of vowels in several morphological forms, in which *patah* (a vowel with no specified length feature) occurs in parallel with *sere* and *holem* (Sarauw 1939, 56–64; Khan 1994b). This applies, for example, to nouns with an originally doubled final consonant. In forms deriving from the *qall* pattern the vowel is *patah*, e.g., רַב [ˈʀaːv] 'much', and in forms deriving from the *qill* and *qull* pattern, the vowel is *sere* and *holem*, respectively, e.g., לֵב [ˈleːv] 'heart', עֹז [ˈʕoːz] 'strength'. Such words would all have a vowel of unspecified length on the phonological level, namely /ˈrav/, /ˈlev/, /ˈʕoz/, and the length would have been a consequence of stress. There is, therefore, no discrepancy in their pattern. The same applies to the underlying phonological representation of the *patah, sere,* and *holem* in verbal forms (קָטַל /qɔṭal/, קָטֵל /qɔṭel/, קָטֹל /qɔṭol/; יְקַטַל /yiqtal/, יְקַטֵל /yiqtel/, יְקַטֹל /yiqtol/) and in segholate nouns (נַעַר /naʿar/, סֵפֶר /sefɛr/, קֹדֶשׁ /qoðɛš/), which would have the phonemes /a/, /e/ and /o/.

In syllables that do not have the main stress the vowels /e/ and /o/ are generally realized phonetically as [ɛ] or [ɔ], respectively, which overlap in quality with the phonemes /ɛ/ and /ɔ/, e.g., וַיֵּרֶד /vayˈyēreð/ [vayˈyeːʀeð] 'and he came down', קֳדָשִׁים /qoðɔ̄ˈʃīm/ [qɔðɔːˈʃiːm] 'holy things'. A second-

---

[93] Syllables in the Tiberian reading tradition are in principle bimoraic (see Khan 2013c for further details).

ary stress may be marked on short [ɔ] and lengthen it to [ɔː], as in קֳדָשִׁים [ˌqɔːðɔːˈʃiːm] 'holy things' (Exod. 29.37). The underlying phonemic representation of a word such as צֱרִי [ṣɔˈʀiː] 'balm' would be /ṣoˈrī/, the pausal form of which would be צֳרִי [ˈṣoːʀiː] with primary stress on the first syllable (attested in Rabbinic Hebrew).

In principle, all the phonemes /a/, /ɛ/, /i/, /u/, /e/, and /o/, which synchronically in the medieval Tiberian reading tradition should be analyzed as lacking a feature of length in their specification, correspond to vowels that were short in all contexts at an earlier historical period. With regard to the vowels that synchronically should be analyzed as having a length feature (i.e., /ɔ̄/, /ō/, /ē/, /ū/, /ī/), these mostly corresponded to historically long vowels, with the exception of /ɔ̄/, which resulted from the historical lengthening of an original short *a, and /ē/, which in some cases developed from the historical lengthening of an original short *i.

The distinction between vowels that are inherently long and those that are long through prosodic stress was already adumbrated by medieval scholars, in particular Ḥayyūj and Judah Ha-Levi (Steiner 2001).

Epenthetic vowels, i.e. vowels marked by vocalic *shewa* or variants of this marked by *ḥateph* vowels, should not be represented at a phonological level, e.g. מְלָכִים /mlɔ̄ˈχīm/ [malɔːˈχiːm], יִשְׁמְרוּ /yiʃmˈrū/ [jiʃmaˈʀuː] 'they guard', יַעֲשׂוּ /yaʕˈsū/ [jaːʕaˈsuː] 'they do'. It follows from this that secondary stress must be assigned after the insertion of epenthetics at the phonetic level.

It is necessary to distinguish long vowel phonemes and vowel phonemes of unspecified length at a phonological level to derive the length distinction in pairs such as אָכְלָה /ʔχˈlɔ̄/ [ʔɔχˈlɔː] 'food' versus אָכְלָה /ʔɔ̄χˈlɔ̄/ [ˌʔɔːχˈlɔː] 'she ate', and יִרְאוּ /yirˈʔū/ [jiʀˈʔuː] 'they see' versus יִרְאוּ /yīrˈʔū/ [jiːiʀˈʔuː] 'they fear'.

11. CONCLUDING REMARKS AND SELECTED READING

In what precedes, we have examined the components of the Tiberian Masoretic tradition. These consist of the Tiberian reading tradition and seven written components that appear in the Tiberian Masoretic Bible manuscripts, i.e. the consonantal text, the layout of the text, the paragraph divisions, the accent signs, the vocalization, the marginal notes and the Masoretic treatises. After the activity of the Masoretes had ceased, the written components were transmitted by scribes but the Tiberian reading tradition was soon forgotten and the Tiberian Masoretic text was read in Jewish communities with other reading traditions.

The written components, apart from the Masoretic treatises and the Masoretic notes, represent ancient traditions most of which can be traced back hundreds of years before the Masoretes into the Second Temple period. The same applies to the Tiberian reading tradition. Some elements of the Masoretic notes can be traced to the Talmudic period. The various components constituted closely related but to some extent independent layers of tradition which were not completely harmonized with each other. This lack of harmonization reflects the precision with which they were transmitted over the centuries.

SELECTED GENERAL READING

Consonantal Text

Barthélemy, Dominique. 1982. *Critique Textuelle De l'Ancien Testament.* Orbis biblicus et orientalis 50. Fribourg, Suisse : Göttingen: Éditions universitaires ; Vandenhoeck & Ruprecht.

Cross, Frank M., and Shemaryahu Talmon, eds. 1976. *Qumran and the History of the Biblical Text.* Cambridge, Mass. ; London: Harvard University Press.

Deist, Ferdinand. 1981. *Towards the Text of the Old Testament.* Trans. Walter K. Winckler. 2nd ed. Pretoria: DR Church Bookseller.

Mulder, Martin J. 1988. "The transmission of the Biblical text." In *Mikra: Text, Translation, Reading and Interpretation of the Hebrew Bible in Ancient Judaism and Early Christianity,* ed. Martin J. Mulder, 87–135. Compendia rerum Iudaicarum ad Novum Testamentum 1. Assen: Van Gorcum.

Talmon, Shemaryahu. 1970. "The Old Testament text." In *The Cambridge History of the Bible,* ed. Peter R Ackroyd and C. F Evans, 159–199. Cambridge: Cambridge University Press.

Tov, Emanuel. 1992. *Textual Criticism of the Hebrew Bible.* Minneapolis, Minn: Fortress Press.

———. 1997. *The Text-Critical Use of the Septuagint in Biblical Research.* 2nd ed. Jerusalem biblical studies 8. Jerusalem: Simor.

Würthwein, Ernst. 1988. *Der Text des Alten Testaments: Eine Einführung in die Biblia Hebraica.* 5th ed. Stuttgart: Deutsche Bibelgesellschaft.

Ulrich, Eugene. 2013. "The Old Testament text and its transmission." In *The New Cambridge History. From the Beginnings to 600,* eds. James Carleton Paget and Joachim Schaper, 83–104. Cambridge: Cambridge University Press.

Layout of the Text and Codicology

Breuer, Mordechai. 1977. *The Aleppo Codex and the Accepted Version of the Bible.* Jerusalem: Mosad ha-Rav Kook, 149–189 (in Hebrew).

Olszowy-Schlanger, Judith. 2012. "The Hebrew Bible." In *The New Cambridge History of the Bible. Vol. 2. From 600 to 1450,* ed. Richard Marsden and E. Ann Matter, 19–40. Cambridge: Cambridge University Press.

Yeivin, Israel. 1980. *Introduction to the Tiberian Masorah.* Trans. E. J Revell. Masoretic studies no. 5. Missoula: Scholars Press, 43–44.

Marking of Paragraphs

Ginsburg, Christian D. 1966. *Introduction to the Massoretico-Critical Edition of the Hebrew Bible*. Reprint. New York: Ktav.

Korpel, Marjo C. A, Josef M Oesch, and Stanley E Porter, eds. 2007. *Method in Unit Delimitation*. Pericope : scripture as written and read in antiquity v. 6. Leiden, The Netherlands ; Boston: Brill.

Maori, Yeshayahu. 1982. "The tradition of Pisqaʾot in ancient Hebrew MSS – The Isaiah texts and commentaries from Qumran." *Textus* 10: 1–50 (Hebrew section).

Oesch, Josef M. 1979. *Petucha Und Setuma: Untersuchungen Zu Einer Überlieferten Gliederung Im Hebräischen Text Des Alten Testaments*. Orbis biblicus et orientalis 27. Freiburg, Schweiz : Göttingen: Universitätsverlag ; Vandenhoeck & Ruprecht.

Perrot, Charles. 1969. "Petuhot et Setumot, étude sur les alinéas du Pentateuque." *Revue Biblique* 76: 50–91.

Yeivin, Israel. 1969. "The division into sections of the book of Psalms." *Textus* 7: 76–102.

Accents

Cohen, Miles B. 1969. *The System of Accentuation in the Hebrew Bible*. Minneapolis: Milco Press.

Freedman, David B. and Miles B. Cohen. 1974. "The Masoretes as Exegetes: Selected Examples." In *1972 and 1972 Proeceedings*, ed. Harry M. Orlinksy, 35–46. Masoretic Studies 1. Missoula, Montana: Scholars Press.

Kogut, Simcha. 1994. *Correlations between Biblical Accentuation and Traditional Jewish Exegesis. Linguistic and Contextual Studies*. Sidrat sefarim le-ḥeḳer ha-Miḳra mi-yisudo shel S. Sh. Peri. Jerusalem: Magnes, The Hebrew University (in Hebrew).

Wickes, William. 1881. *A Treatise on the Accentuation of the Three so-Called Poetical Books of the Old Testament, Psalms, Proverbs, and Job.* Oxford: Clarendon Press.

———. 1887. *A Treatise on the Accentuation of the Twenty-One so-Called Prose Books of the Old Testament: With a Facsimile of a Page of the Codex Assigned to Ben-Asher in Aleppo.* Oxford: Clarendon Press.

Yeivin, Israel. 1980. *Introduction to the Tiberian Masorah.* Trans. E. J Revell. Masoretic studies no. 5. Missoula: Scholars Press.

Vocalization and Reading Tradition

Chiesa, Bruno. 1979. *The Emergence of Hebrew Biblical Pointing: The Indirect Sources.* Judentum und Umwelt 1. Frankfurt: Lang.

Grabbe, Lester L. 1977. *Comparative Philology and the Text of Job: A Study in Methodology.* Dissertation series / Society of Biblical Literature no. 34. Missoula, Montana: Scholars Press, for the Society of Biblical Literature, 179–197.

Khan, Geoffrey. 1996. "The Tiberian Pronunciation Tradition of Biblical Hebrew." *Zeitschrift für Althebraïstik* 9: 1–23.

———. 2013d. "Biblical Hebrew: Pronunciation Traditions." In *Encyclopedia of Hebrew Language and Linguistics,* ed. Geoffrey Khan, Shmuel Bolozky, Steven E. Fassberg, Gary A. Rendsburg, Aaron D. Rubin, Ora R. Schwarzwald and Tamar Zewi, vol. 1, 341–352. Leiden— Boston: Brill.

Morag, Shelomo. 1962. *The Vocalization Systems of Arabic, Hebrew, and Aramaic: Their Phonetic and Phonemic Principles.* Janua linguarum nr. 13. 's-Gravenhage: Mouton.

———. 1974. "On the historical validity of the vocalization of the Hebrew Bible." *Journal of the American Oriental Society* 94: 307–315.

Revell, E. John. 1970a. *Hebrew Texts with Palestinian Vocalization.* Near and Middle East series 7. Toronto: University of Toronto Press.

———. 1970b. "Studies in the Palestinian Vocalization of Hebrew." In *Essays on the Ancient Semitic World*, ed. John. W. Wevers. and Donald. B. Redford, 59–100. Toronto: Toronto University Press.

———. 1977. *Biblical Texts with Palestinian Pointing and Their Accents*. Masoretic studies no. 4. Missoula, Montana: Published by Scholars Press for the Society of Biblical Literature.

Schorch, Stefan. 2004. *Die Vokale des Gesetzes: Die Samaritanische Lesetradition als Textzeugin der Tora* (Beihefte zur Zeitschrift für die Alttestamentliche Wissenschaft 339). Berlin: de Gruyter.

Yeivin, Israel. 1985. *The Hebrew Language Tradition as Reflected in the Babylonian Vocalization*. Jerusalem: The Academy of the Hebrew Language.

Masoretic Notes and Treatises

Dotan, Aron. 1971. "The Masorah." *Encyclopaedia Judaica*. Jerusalem–New York: MacMillan.

Kelley, Page H, Daniel S Mynatt, and Timothy G Crawford. 1998. *The Masorah of Biblia Hebraica Stuttgartensia: Introduction and Annotated Glossary*. Grand Rapids, Mich: W.B. Eerdmans.

Yeivin, Israel. 1980. *Introduction to the Tiberian Masorah*. Masoretic Studies. Missoula: Scholars Press.

Masorah and Grammar

Dotan, Aron. 1990. "De la Massora à la grammaire. Les débuts de la pensée grammaticale dans l'hébreu." *Journal Asiatique* 278: 13–30.

Khan, Geoffrey. 2000. *The Early Karaite Tradition of Hebrew Grammatical Thought: Including a Critical Edition, Translation and Analysis of the Diqduq of ʾAbū Yaʿqūb Yūsuf ibn Nūḥ on the Hagiographa*. Studies in Semitic Languages and Linguistics. Leiden: Brill. Introduction.

REFERENCES

Albrektson, Bertil. 1978. "Reflections on the emergence of a standard text of the Hebrew Bible." In *Congress volume*, 49–65. Vetus Testamentum Supplement 29. Leiden: Brill.

Albright, William F. 1955. "New light on early recensions of the Hebrew Bible." *Bulletin of the American Schools of Oriental Research* 140: 27–33.

Alexander, Philip. 1988. "Jewish Aramaic translations of Hebrew scriptures." In *Mikra: Text, Translation, Reading and Interpretation of the Hebrew Bible in Ancient Judaism and Early Christianity*, ed. Martin J. Mulder, 217–253. Compendia rerum Iudaicarum ad Novum Testamentum 1. Assen: Van Gorcum.

Allony, Nehemiah. 1964a. "רשימת מונחים קראים מהמאה השמינית." In כתבי החברה לחקר המקרא בישראל לזכר ד"ר י.פ. קורנגרין ז"ל, ed. Asher Weiser and Ben-Zion Luria, 324–63. Tel-Aviv: Niv.

———. 1964b. "ספר הקולות — כתאב אלמצוותאת למשה בן אשר." *Lešonénu* 29: 9–23, 136–159.

———. 1965. "סדר הסימנים." *Hebrew Union College Annual* 35: 1–40 (Hebrew section).

———. 1973. "עלי בן יהודה הנזיר וחיבור יסודות הלשון העברית." *Lešonénu* 34: 75–105, 187–205.

Alvestad, Silje, and Lutz Edzard. 2009. *La-ḥšōḇ but La-ḥăzōr?: Sonority, Optimality, and the Hebrew פ"ח Forms*. Abhandlungen für die Kunde des Morgenlandes Bd. 66. Wiesbaden: Harrassowitz.

Andersen, Francis I, and A. Dean Forbes. 1986. *Spelling in the Hebrew Bible: Dahood Memorial Lecture*. Biblica et orientalia 41. Rome: Biblical Institute Press.

Aptowitzer, Victor. 1970. *Das Schriftwort in der Rabbinischen Literatur*. The Library of Biblical Studies. New York: Ktav Publishing House.

Ariel, Chanan. 2013. "Orthography: Biblical Hebrew." In *Encyclopedia of Hebrew Language and Linguistics*, ed. Geoffrey Khan, Shmuel Bolozky, Steven E. Fassberg, Gary A. Rendsburg, Aaron D. Rubin, Ora R. Schwarzwald and Tamar Zewi, vol. 2, 940–948. Leiden—Boston: Brill.

Bacher, Wilhelm. 1895. "Le Grammairien Anonyme de Jérusalem." *Revue Des Études Juives* 30: 232–256.

———. 1899. *Die Exegetische Terminologie der Jüdischen Traditionsliteratur*. Leipzig: Hinrichs.

———. 1974. *Die Anfänge der Hebräischen Grammatik; and die Hebräische Sprachwissenschaft vom 10. bis zum 16. Jahrhundert*. Amsterdam studies in the theory and history of linguistic science v. 4. Amsterdam: J. Benjamins.

Baer, Seligmann, and Hermann Leberecht Strack. 1879. *Diḳduḳe Ha-Ṭeʿamim*. Leipzig: L. Pernoy.

Barkay, Gabriel. 1989. "The priestly benediction of the Ketef Hinnom plaques." *Cathedra* 52: 37–76.

Barr, James. 1968. *Comparative Philology and the Text of the Old Testament*. Oxford: Clarendon P.

———. 1981. "A new look at the kethib-qere." *Oudtestamentische Studien* 21: 19–37.

———. 1984. "Migraš in the Old Testament." *Journal of Semitic Studies* 29: 15–31.

———. 1990. "Guessing in the Septuagint." In *Studien Zur Septuaginta, Robert Hanhart Zu Ehren: Aus Anlass Seines 65. Geburtstages*, ed. Detlef Fraenkel, U. Quast, and John William Wevers, 19–34. Mitteilungen des Septuaginta-Unternehmens 20. Göttingen: Vandenhoeck & Ruprecht.

Beit-Arié, Malachi. 1993. *Hebrew Manuscripts of East and West: Towards a Comparative Codicology*. The Panizzi lectures 1992. London: British Library.

Beit-Arié, Malachi, Colette Sirat, Mordechai Glatzer, and Comité de paléographie hébraïque. 1997. *Codices Hebraicis Litteris Exarati Quo Tempore Scripti Fuerint Exhibentes*. Monumenta palaeographica Medii Aevi. Series Hebraica. Turnhout : Paris : Jérusalem: Brepols ; Institut de recherche et d'histoire des textes, CNRS ; Académie nationale des sciences et des lettres d'Israël.

Ben David, Abba. 1957. "ʿAl ma naḥlequ Ben-ʾAšer u-Ben-Naphtali." *Tarbiz* 26: 384–409.

Ben-David, Israel. 1995. *Contextual and pausal forms in Biblical Hebrew*. Jerusalem: Magnes Press, Hebrew University (in Hebrew).

Ben-Ḥayyim, Zeev. 1957. "מסורה ומסורת." *Lešonénu* 21: 283–292.

———. 1958. "The Samaritan tradition and its relationship to the language tradition of the Dead Sea scrolls and to Rabbinic Hebrew." *Lešonénu* 22: 223–245 (in Hebrew).

Ben-Ḥayyim, Zeev, and Abraham Tal. 2000. *A Grammar of Samaritan Hebrew: Based on the Recitation of the Law in Comparison with the Tiberian and Other Jewish Traditions*. Rev. ed. in English. Jerusalem: Winona Lake, Ind: Hebrew University Magnes Press ; Eisenbrauns.

Berliner, Abraham. 1872. *Pletath Soferim: Beiträge zur Jüdischen Schriftauslegung im Mittelalter nebst Midrasch über die Grunde der Defectiva und Plena*. Breslau: Schletter.

Boyarin, Daniel. 1978. "On the history of the Babylonian Jewish Aramaic reading traditions: The reflexes of *a and *ā." *Journal of Near Eastern Studies* 37: 141–160.

———. 1988. "Towards the Talmudic lexicon IV." *Studies in Hebrew and Arabic in memory of Dov Eron* (Teʿuda 6), ed. by Aron Dotan, 63–75. Tel-Aviv: Tel-Aviv University.

Breuer, Mordechai. 1977–1982. תורה, נביאים, כתובים, מוגהים על פי הנוסח והמסורה : מוגהים על פי הנוסח והמסורה של 3 כתר ארם צובה, וכתבי יד הקרובים לו. 3 vols. Jerusalem: Mosad ha-Rav Kook.

Brønno, Einar. 1943. *Studien über Hebräische Morphologie und Vokalismus Auf Grundlage der Mercatischen Fragmente der Zweiten Kolumne der Hexapla des Origenes.* Abhandlungen für die Kunde des Morgenlandes 28. Leipzig: F. A. Brockhaus.

Busi, Giulio. 1984. *Horayat Ha-qore>: Una Grammatica Ebraica Del Secolo XI.* Judentum Und Umwelt 11. Frankfurt am Main: Peter Lang.

Cohen, Maimon. 2007. *The Kethiḇ and Qeri System in the Biblical Text: A Linguistic Analysis of the Various Traditions Based on the Manuscript "Keter Aram Tsova".* Jerusalem: Magnes Press, Hebrew University.

Cohen, Menahem. 1987. "Subsystems of Tiberian 'Extramasoretic' accentuation and the extent of their distribution in mediaeval Biblical manuscripts." *Lešonénu* 51: 188–206 (in Hebrew).

Cohen, Menahem ed. 1992–. *Miqra>ot Gedolot "Ha-Keter": A revised and augmented scientific edition miqra>ot gedolot based on the Aleppo Codex and early medieval manuscripts.* Ramat Gan: Bar-Ilan University Press.

Cook, Stanley A. 1903. "A pre-massoretic biblical papyrus." *Proceedings of the Society of Biblical Archaeology* 25: 34–56.

Cross, Frank M. 1976. The evolution of a theory of local texts. In *Qumran and the History of the Biblical Text,* ed. Frank M. Cross and Shemaryahu Talmon, 306–320. Cambridge, MA—London: Harvard University Press.

Cross, Frank M., and David N. Freedman. 1952. *Early Hebrew Orthography: A Study of the Epigraphic Evidence.* American Oriental series v. 36. New Haven: American Oriental Society.

DeCaen, Vincent. 2003. "Hebrew sonority and Tiberian contact anaptyxis: the case of verbs primæ gutturalis." *Journal of Semitic Studies* 48 (1): 35–46.

Delcor, Mathias. 1968. "Le Temple d'Onias en Égypte." *Revue Biblique* 75: 188–203.

Derenbourg, Joseph. 1871. *Manuel du lecteur, d'un auteur inconnu : publié d'après un manuscrit venu du Yémen et accompagné de notes.* Paris: Imprimerie nationale.

———. 1886. *Le Livre des Parterres Fleuris: Grammaire Hébraïque en Arabe d'Abou 'l-Walid Merwan Ibn Djanah De Cordoue.* Paris: F. Vieweg.

Díaz Esteban, Fernando. 1975. *Sefer ʾOklah wĕ-ʾOklah: Colección de Listas de Palabras Destinadas a Conservar la Integridad del Texto Hebreo de la Biblia entre los Judios de la Edad Media.* Textos y estudios "Cardenal Cisneros" 4. Madrid: Consejo Superior de Investigaciones Científicas.

Díez Macho, Alejandro. 1971. *Manuscritos Hebreos y Arameos De la Biblia: Contribución al Estudio de las Diversas Tradiciones del Tecto del Antiguo Testamento.* Roma: Institutum patristicum Augustinianum.

Dotan, Aron. 1967. *The Diqduqé Haṭṭĕʿamim of Ahăron ben Moše ben Ašér.* Jerusalem: The Academy of the Hebrew Language.

———. 1971. "The Masorah." *Encyclopaedia Judaica.* Jerusalem—New York: MacMillan.

———. 1973. תורה נביאים וכתובים מדויקים הטיב על פי הניקוד הטעמים והמסורה של אהרון בן משה בן אשר בכתב יד לנינגרד. Tel-Aviv: ʿAdi.

———. 1990. "De la Massora à la grammaire. Les débuts de la pensée grammaticale dans l'hébreu." *Journal Asiatique* 278: 13–30.

———. 1997. *Dawn of Hebrew Linguistics: The Book of Elegance of the Language of the Hebrews.* Jerusalem: ha-Iggud ha-ʿOlami le-Madaʿe ha-Yahadut.

———. 2001. *Biblia Hebraica Leningradensia: Prepared according to the Vocalization, Accents, and Masora of Aaron Ben Moses Ben Asher in the Leningrad Codex.* Leiden ; Boston: Brill.

Drory, Rina. 1988. *The Emergence of Jewish-Arabic Literary Contacts at the Beginnig of the Tenth Century.* Literature, Meaning, Culture 17. Tel-Aviv: Tel-Aviv University (in Hebrew).

118   REFERENCES

Dukes, Leopold. 1845. קונטרס המסורה המיוחס לבן־אשר ונלוו אליו איזה העתקות
מפירוש ספר יצירה לר׳ יעקוב בן נסים. Tübingen: L. F. Fues.

Eldar, Ilan. 1978. *The Hebrew Language Tradition in Medieval Ashkenaz (ca.
940–1350 C.E.).* ʿEdah ve-Lashon. Jerusalem: Magnes (in Hebrew).

————. 1980a. "On Ben-Asher and Ben-Naphtali." *Lěšonénu* 45: 311–313 (in
Hebrew).

————. 1980b. "Bāb maḥāll al-ḥurūf from Kitāb Hidāyat al-Qāri: Critically
edited with Hebrew translation, commentary and introduction."
Lešonénu 45: 233–259 (in Hebrew).

————. 1984a. "The double pronunciation of the Tiberian reš." *Lešonénu* 48–
49: 22–34 (in Hebrew).

————. 1984b. "חוק אוי״ה ובגדכפת." *Hebrew Union College Annual* 55: 1–14.

————. 1986. "האמנם נמצאו בגניזה החיבורים האבודים כתאב אלמצוותאת, ניקוד ר׳
סעדיה, מחברת עלי בן יהודה הנזיר?" *Alei Sefer* 12: 51–61.

————. 1988. "The Treatise on the Shewa and 'Seder Ha-Simanim'—Two
Parts of a Whole." In *Studies in Hebrew and Arabic in Memory of Dov
Eron*, edited by Aron Dotan, 127–138. Teʿuda 6. Tel-Aviv: Tel-Aviv
University (in Hebrew).

————. 1994. *The Study of the Art of Correct Reading as Reflected in the Medieval Treatise Hidāyat al-Qāri*. Jerusalem: Academy of the Hebrew
Language (in Hebrew).

Engel, Edna. 1999. "Styles of Hebrew script in the tenth and eleventh centuries in the light of dated and datable Geniza documents." *Teʿuda* 15:
365–412 (in Hebrew).

Fassberg, Steven. 1989. "The origin of the ketib/qere in the Aramaic portions of Ezra and Daniel." *Vetus Testamentum* 39: 1–12.

————. 1991. *A Grammar of the Palestinian Targum Fragments from the Cairo
Genizah*. Harvard Semitic Studies no. 38. Atlanta, GA: Scholars
Press.

Filipowski, Herschell E. 1854. *Maḥberet Menaḥem*. London: Ḥevrat meʿorere
yeshenim.

Fishbane, Michael A. 1985. *Biblical Interpretation in Ancient Israel*. Oxford: Clarendon.

———. 1988. "Use, authority and interpretation of Mikra at Qumran." In *Mikra: Text, Translation, Reading and Interpretation of the Hebrew Bible in Ancient Judaism and Early Christianity*, ed. Martin J. Mulder, 339–377. Compendia rerum Iudaicarum ad Novum Testamentum 1. Assen: Van Gorcum.

Frensdorff, Salomon. 1864. ספר אכלה ואכלה והוא חיבור מהמסורה הגדולה נמצא בכ״י ישן בבית אוצר הספרים של הקיסר בעיר פאריס. Hannover: Hahn.

Friedman, Matti. 2012. *The Aleppo Codex: a True Story of Obsession, Faith, and the Pursuit of an Ancient Bible*. Chapel Hill, NC: Algonquin Books of Chapel Hill.

Garbell, Irene. 1964. "'Flat' words and syllables in Jewish East New Aramaic of Persian Azerbaijan and the contiguous districts (a problem of multilingualism)." In *Studies in Egyptology and linguistics in honour of Hans Jakob Polotsky*, ed. Haiim Rosén, 86–103. Jerusalem: Israel Exploration Society.

Ginsberg, Harold L. 1934. "From behind the Massorah." *Tarbiz* 5: 208–223 (in Hebrew).

Ginsburg, Christian D. 1966. *Introduction to the Massoretico-Critical Edition of the Hebrew Bible*. Reprint. New York: Ktav.

———. 1975. *The Massorah*. The Library of Biblical Studies. Reprint. New York: Ktav.

Glatzer, Mordechai. 1989. "The Aleppo Codex—codicological and paleographical aspects." *Sefonot* 4: 167–276 (in Hebrew).

Goldschmidt, Ernst D. 1960. *The Passover Haggadah: its Sources and History*. Jerusalem: Bialik Institute (in Hebrew).

Gordis, Robert. 1971. *The Biblical Text in the Making; a Study of the Kethib-Qere*. Augm. ed. New York: Ktav.

Goshen-Gottstein, Moshe. 1960. "The authenticity of the Aleppo codex." *Textus* 1: 17–58.

———. 1962. "Biblical manuscripts in the United States." *Textus* 2: 28–59.

————. 1976. כתר ארם צובא: מסרו ונקדו ר' אהרון בן אשר. Jerusalem: Magnes, Hebrew University.

Grossberg, Manasseh. 1902. ספר יצירה המיוחס לאברהם אבינו ... עם פירוש ... אבו סהל דונש בן תמים. London.

Hanson, Richard S. 1964. "Paleo-Hebrew scripts in the Hasmonean ages." *Bulletin of the American Schools of Oriental Research* 175: 26–42.

Harviainen, Tapani. 1977. *On the Vocalism of the Closed Unstressed Syllables in Hebrew: A Study Based on the Evidence Provided by the Transcriptions of St. Jerome and Palestinian Punctuations.* Helsinki: Societas Orientalis Fennica.

Heinemann, Joseph. 1968. "The triennial lectionary cycle." *Journal of Jewish Studies* 19: 41–48.

Hoerning, Reinhart. 1889. *British Museum Karaite MSS. Descriptions and Collation of Six Karaite Manuscripts of Portions of the Hebrew Bible in Arabic Characters; with a Complete Reproduction ... of One, Exodus I. 1 – VIII. 5, in ... Facsimiles.* London.

Hurwitz, Simon ed. 1893. ספרים היוצאים לאור ... מקיצי. מחזור ויטרי לרבנו שמחה נרדמים שנה 9. Berlin: Itzkowski.

Janssens, Gerard 1982. *Studies in Hebrew Historical Linguistics Based on Origen's Secunda.* Orientalia Gandensia 9. Leuven: Uitgeverij Peeters.

Japhet, Sara. 1987. "Interchanges of verbal roots in parallel texts in Chronicles." *Hebrew Studies* 28: 9–50.

Jeffery, Arthur. 1937. *Materials for the History of the Text of the Qurʾān: The Old Codices. The Kitāb Al-Maṣāḥif of Ibn Abī Dawūd, Together with a Collection of the Variant Readings from the Codices of Ibn Maʿsūd, Ubai, ʿAlī, Ibn ʿAbbās, Anas, Abū Mūsā and Other Early Qurʾānic Authorities Which Present a Type of Text Anterior to That of the Canonical Text of ʿUthmān.* Leiden: Brill.

Kahle, Paul. 1927. *Masoreten des Westens.* Texte und Untersuchungen zur vormasoretischen Grammatik des Hebräischen. Stuttgart: W. Kohlhammer.

———. 1951. *Die hebräischen Handschriften aus der Höhle.* Stuttgart: Kohl-hammer.

———. 1959. *The Cairo Geniza.* 2nd ed. Oxford: Blackwell.

Kennicott, Benjamin. 1776. *Vetus Testamentum Hebraicum: Cum Variis Lectionibus.* Oxford: E Typographeo Clarendoniano.

Khan, Geoffrey. 1987. "Vowel length and syllable structure in the Tiberian tradition of Biblical Hebrew." *Journal of Semitic Studies* 32 (1): 23–82.

———. 1989. "The pronunciation of מַה־ before dageš in the medieval Tiberian Hebrew reading tradition." *Journal of Semitic Studies* 34: 433–41.

———. 1990a. "Standardisation and variation in the orthography of Hebrew Bible and Arabic Qurʾān manuscripts." *Manuscripts of the Middle East* 5: 53–58.

———. 1990b. *Karaite Bible Manuscripts from the Cairo Genizah.* Cambridge University Library Genizah Series. Cambridge: Cambridge University Press.

———. 1990c. "The opinions of al-Qirqisānī concerning the text of the Bible and parallel Muslim attitudes towards the text of the Qurʾān." *Jewish Quarterly Review* 81: 59–73.

———. 1991. "The syllabic nature of Tiberian Hebrew vocalization." In *Semitic Studies in Honor of Wolf Leslau,* ed. Alan S Kaye, 850–865. Wiesbaden: Harrassowitz.

———. 1992a. "The medieval Karaite transcriptions of Hebrew in Arabic script." *Israel Oriental Studies* 12: 157–176.

———. 1992b. "The function of the *shewa* sign in vocalized Judaeo-Arabic texts from the Genizah." In *Genizah Research after Ninety Years: The Case of Judaeo-Arabic,* ed. Joshua Blau and Stefan Reif, 105–111. University of Cambridge Oriental Publications 47. Cambridge: Cambridge University Press.

———. 1992c. "The pronunciation of minor *gaᶜya* as reflected by Karaite Bible manuscripts in Arabic transcription." *Meḥqarim ba-Lashon* 5–6: 465–479 (in Hebrew).

———. 1994a. "The pronunciation of the verbs *haya* and *ḥaya* in the Tiberian tradition of Biblical Hebrew." In *Semitic and Cushitic Studies*, ed. Gideon Goldenberg and Shlomo Raz, 133–144. Jerusalem–Wiesbaden: Harrassowitz.

———. 1994b. "The historical background of the vowel ṣere in some Hebrew verbal and nominal forms." *Bulletin of the School of Oriental and African Studies* 57: 133–144.

———. 1995. "The pronunciation of the *reš* in the Tiberian tradition of Biblical Hebrew." *Hebrew Union College Annual* 66: 67–80.

———. 1996a. "*Šewa* and *ḥaṭep* signs in the Tiberian vocalization system." *Journal of Semitic Studies* 41 (1): 65–74.

———. 1996b. "The Tiberian pronunciation tradition of Biblical Hebrew." *Zeitschrift für Althebraïstik* 9: 1–23.

———. 1997. "Jewish Palestinian Aramaic phonology." In *Phonologies of Asia and Africa*, ed. Alan S Kaye, 103–113. Winona Lake: Eisenbrauns.

———. 2000. *The Early Karaite Tradition of Hebrew Grammatical Thought: Including a Critical Edition, Translation and Analysis of the Diqduq of ʾAbū Yaᶜqūb Yūsuf ibn Nūḥ on the Hagiographa*. Studies in Semitic Languages and Linguistics. Leiden: Brill.

———. 2003. "The contribution of the Karaites to the study of the Hebrew language." In *A Guide to Karaite Studies: The History and Literary Sources of Medieval and Modern Karaite Judaism*, ed. Meira Polliack, 291–318. Handbuch der Orientalistik 73. Boston: Brill.

———. 2005. "Some parallels in linguistic development between Biblical Hebrew and Neo-Aramaic." In *Semitic Studies in Honour of Edward Ullendorff*, 84–108. Leiden: Brill.

———. 2009. "The pronunciation of *ga⁽ya* with *šewa.*" In *Mas'at Aharon: Linguistic Studies Presented to Aron Dotan*, ed. Moshe Bar-Asher and Chaim E. Cohen, 3*–18*. Jerusalem: Bialik.

———. 2010. "Vocalised Judaeo-Arabic Manuscripts in the Cairo Genizah." In *"From a Sacred Source": Genizah Studies in Honour of Professor Stefan C. Reif*, ed. Ben Outhwaite and Siam Bhayro, 201–218. Leiden—Boston: Brill.

———. 2013a. *"Resh*: Pre-Modern Hebrew." In *Encyclopedia of Hebrew Language and Linguistics*, ed. Geoffrey Khan, Shmuel Bolozky, Steven E. Fassberg, Gary A. Rendsburg, Aaron D. Rubin, Ora R. Schwarzwald and Tamar Zewi, vol. 3, 384–389. Leiden—Boston: Brill.

———. 2013b. *"Shewa*: Pre-Modern Hebrew." In *Encyclopedia of Hebrew Language and Linguistics*, ed. Geoffrey Khan, Shmuel Bolozky, Steven E. Fassberg, Gary A. Rendsburg, Aaron D. Rubin, Ora R. Schwarzwald and Tamar Zewi, vol. 3, 543–554. Leiden—Boston: Brill.

———. 2013c. "Syllable structure: Biblical Hebrew." In *Encyclopedia of Hebrew Language and Linguistics*, ed. Geoffrey Khan, Shmuel Bolozky, Steven E. Fassberg, Gary A. Rendsburg, Aaron D. Rubin, Ora R. Schwarzwald and Tamar Zewi, vol. 3, 666–676. Leiden—Boston: Brill.

———. 2013d. "Biblical Hebrew: Pronunciation Traditions." In *Encyclopedia of Hebrew Language and Linguistics*, ed. Geoffrey Khan, Shmuel Bolozky, Steven E. Fassberg, Gary A. Rendsburg, Aaron D. Rubin, Ora R. Schwarzwald and Tamar Zewi, vol. 1, 341–352. Leiden—Boston: Brill.

Khan, Geoffrey, María Ángeles Gallego, and Judith Olszowy-Schlanger. 2003. *The Karaite Tradition of Hebrew Grammatical Thought in Its Classical Form: A Critical Edition and English Translation of Al-Kitāb Al-Kāfī Fī Al-Luġa Al-'Ibrāniyya by 'Abū Al-Faraj Hārūn Ibn Al-Faraj*. Studies in Semitic Languages and Linguistics 37. Leiden: Brill.

Kutscher, Edward Y. 1965. "Contemporary studies in North-Western Semitic." *Journal of Semitic Studies* 10 (1): 21–51.

———. 1968. "Articulation of the vowels *u, i* in transcriptions of Biblical Hebrew, in Galilean Aramaic and in Mishnaic Hebrew." In *Benjamin de Vries memorial volume: studies presented by colleagues and pupils,* ed. Ezra Zion Melamed, 218–251. Tel-Aviv: Tel-Aviv University.

———. 1979. *The Language and Linguistic Background of the Isaiah Scroll (1 Q Is A).* Studies on the texts of the desert of Judah 6a. Leiden: Brill.

———. 1982. *A History of the Hebrew Language.* Jerusalem: Magnes.

Lambert, Mayer. 1891. *Commentaire Sur Le Séfer Yesira, Ou Livre De La Création.* Paris: É. Bouillon.

Leiman, Shnayer Z. 1976. *The Canonization of Hebrew Scripture: The Talmudic and Midrashic Evidence.* Hamden, Conn: Published for the Academy by Archon Books.

Levy, Kurt. 1936. *Zur Masoretischen Grammatik.* Bonner orientalistische Studien. Stuttgart: Kohlhammer.

Lieberman, Saul. 1962. *Hellenism in Jewish Palestine; Studies in the Literary Transmission, Beliefs and Manners of Palestine in the I Century B.C.E.– IV Century C. E.* 2nd ed. Texts and studies of the Jewish Theological Seminary of America v. 18. New York: Jewish Theological Seminary of America.

Lipshütz, Lazar. 1965. *Kitāb al-Khilaf: Mishael ben Uzziel's Treatise on the Differences between Ben Asher and Ben Naphtali.* Jerusalem: Magnes.

Loewinger, David S. (ed.). 1970. תורה נביאים וכתובים: כתב־יד לנינגרד ב19א, כתב־היד השלם הקדום ביותר של המקרא. Jerusalem: Maqor.

Mann, Jacob. 1926. "On the Terminology of the Early Massorites and Grammarians." In *Oriental Studies Published in Commemoration of the Fortieth Anniversary (1883–1923) of Paul Haupt as Director of the Oriental Seminary of the Johns Hopkins University,* edited by Cyrus Adler and Aaron Ember, 437–445. Baltimore: Johns Hopkins Press.

———. 1972. *Texts and Studies in Jewish History and Literature.* New York: Ktav.

McCarthy, Carmel. 1981. *The Tiqqune Sopherim and Other Theological Correc-tions in the Masoretic Text of the Old Testament.* Orbis biblicus et ori-entalis 36. Freiburg, Schweiz: Universitätsverlag.

Mercerus, Johannes ed. 1978. *Sefer Ṭaʿāme ha-Miqra.* facsimile of 1565 edi-tion. Jerusalem: Makor.

Morag, Shelomo. 1960. ספר טור סיני מוגש לכבוד נ.ה. טור ‏In‏ .שבע כפולות בגדכפר׳׳ת‏ סיני למלאת לו שבעים שנה, ed. Menahem Haran and Ben-Tsiyon Lurya, 207–242. Jerusalem: Kiryat Sepher.

———. 1974. "On the historical validity of the vocalization of the Hebrew Bible." *Journal of the American Oriental Society* 94: 307–315.

———. 1988. *Babylonian Aramaic. The Yemenite tradition.* Jerusalem: Ben-Zvi Institute.

———. 2003. *Studies in Hebrew.* Edited by Moshe Bar-Asher, Yochanan Breuer, and Aharon Maman. Jerusalem: Hebrew University Magnes Press.

Moran, William L. 1961. "The Hebrew language in its Northwest Semitic background." In *The Bible and the Ancient Near East: Essays in Hon-our of William Foxwell Albright*, ed. George E. Wright, 54–72. Garden City-London: Doubleday.

Morrow, William S., and Ernest G. Clarke. 1986. "The ketib/qere in the Aramaic portions of Ezra and Daniel." *Vetus Testamentum* 36: 406–422.

Narkiss, Bezalel. 1969. *Hebrew Illuminated Manuscripts.* Jerusalem—New York: Macmillan.

Naveh, Joseph. 1970. *The Development of the Aramaic Script.* Proceedings of the Israel Academy of Sciences and Humanities 5/1. Jerusalem: Is-rael Academy of Sciences and Humanities.

Neubauer, Adolf. 1891. *Petite grammaire hébraïque provenant de Yemen texte arabe, publié d'après les manuscrits connus.* Leipzig: Harrassowitz.

Nöldeke, Theodor. 1868. *Die Alttestamentliche Literatur in einer Reihe von Aufsätzen.* Leipzig: Quandt & Händel.

Nyberg, Henrik S. 1934. "Das textkritische Problem des Alten Testaments." *Zeitschrift für die Alttestamentliche Wissenschaft* 11: 241–254.

Oesch, Josef M. 1979. *Petucha und Setuma: Untersuchungen zu einer Überlieferten Gliederung im Hebräischen Text des Alten Testaments*. Orbis biblicus et orientalis 27. Freiburg, Schweiz : Göttingen: Universitätsverlag ; Vandenhoeck & Ruprecht.

Ofer, Yosef. 2001. *Babylonian Masora of the Pentateuch, its Principles and Methods*. Jerusalem: Academy of the Hebrew Language (in Hebrew).

Ognibeni, Bruno. 1995. *La Seconda Parte del Sefer ʾOklah weʾOklah: Edizione del Ms. Halle, Universitätsbibliothek Y B 4o 10, Ff. 68–124*. Textos y estudios "Cardenal Cisneros" 57. Madrid : Fribourg: Instituto de Filología del CSIC, Departamento de Filología Bíblica y de Oriente Antiguo ; Université Fribourg.

Olszowy-Schlanger, Judith. 2012. "The Hebrew Bible." In *The New Cambridge History of the Bible. Vol. 2. From 600 to 1450*, ed. Richard Marsden and E. Ann Matter, 19–40. Cambridge: Cambridge University Press.

Orlinksy, Harry M. 1960. "The origin of the kethib-qere system—a new approach." In *Congress volume*, 184–192. Supplements to Vetus Testamentum 7. Leiden: Brill.

Penkower, Jordan S. 1981. "Maimonides and the Aleppo codex." *Textus* 9: 39–128.

———. 1983. "Bomberg's first Bible edition and the beginning of his printing press." *Kiryat Sefer* 58: 586–604 (in Hebrew).

Perrot, Charles. 1988. "The reading of the Bible in the ancient synagogue." In *Mikra: Text, Translation, Reading and Interpretation of the Hebrew Bible in Ancient Judaism and Early Christianity*, ed. Martin J. Mulder, 137–159. Compendia rerum Iudaicarum ad Novum Testamentum 1. Assen: Van Gorcum.

Qimron, Elisha. 1986. *The Hebrew of the Dead Sea Scrolls*. Atlanta, GA: Scholars.

Qirqisānī, Ya'qūb ibn Isḥāq. 1939. *Kitab Al-Anwār w-al-Marāqib*. Ed. Leon Nemoy. New York: The Alexander Kohut memorial foundation.

Revell, E. John. 1971. "The oldest evidence for the Hebrew accent system." *Bulletin of the John Rylands Library* 54: 214–222.

———. 1977. *Biblical Texts with Palestinian Pointing and Their Accents*. Masoretic studies no. 4. Missoula, Montana: Published by Scholars Press for the Society of Biblical Literature.

———. 1980. "Pausal forms in Biblical Hebrew, their function, origin and significance." *Journal of Semitic Studies* 25: 165–179.

Ringgren, Helmer. 1949. "Oral transmission and written transmission in the Old Testament. Some observations." *Studia Theologica* 3: 34–59.

Roberts, Bleddyn Jones. 1951. *The Old Testament Text and Versions; the Hebrew Text in Transmission and the History of the Ancient Versions*. Cardiff: University of Wales Press.

Roman, André. 1983. *Étude de la Phonologie et de la Morphologie de la Koine Arabe*. 2 vols. Aix-en-Provence: Université de Provence.

Rossi, Giovanni B. de. 1784–1799. *Variae Lectiones Veteris Testamenti: 4 Tomi Et Supplement*. Parma.

Sáenz-Badillos, Angel. 1980. *Tešubot de Dunaš Ben Labrat*. Granada: Univ. de Granada.

———. 1996. *A History of the Hebrew Language*. Trans. John Ewolde. Cambridge: Cambridge University Press.

Sarauw, Christian Preben Emil. 1939. *Über Akzent und Silbenbildung in den Älteren Semitischen Sprachen* (Historisk-filologiske Meddelelser, Det Kgl. Danske Videnskabernes Selskab 26, 8). Copenhagen: Ejnar Munksgaard.

Schorch, Stefan. 2004. *Die Vokale des Gesetzes: Die Samaritanische Lesetradition als Textzeugin der Tora* (Beihefte zur Zeitschrift für die Alttestamentliche Wissenschaft 339). Berlin: de Gruyter.

Schreiner, Martin. 1886. "Zur Geschichte der Aussprache des Hebräischen." *Zeitschrift für die alttestamentliche Wissenschaft* 6: 213–259.

Shamosh, Amnon. 1987. *Ha-Keter: The Story of the Aleppo Codex.* Jerusalem: Ben-Zvi Institute (in Hebrew).

Shoshany, Ronit. 2003. *Babylonian Accentuation System: Rules of Division and Accentuation, Stages of Development, and Relationship to the Tiberian System.* Ph.D. thesis, Tel-Aviv: Tel-Aviv University (in Hebrew).

Siegfried, Carl. 1884. "Die Aussprache des Hebräischen bei Hieronymus." *Zeitschrift für die Alttestamentliche Wissenschaft* 4: 34–83.

Sirat, Colette. 1985. *Les Papyrus en Caractères Hébraïques Trouvés En Égypte.* Paris: Centre National de la Recherche Scientifique.

Skoss, Solomon L. 1936–1945. *The Hebrew-Arabic Dictionary of the Bible, Known as Kitāb Jāmiʿ Al-Alfāẓ (Agrōn) of David Ben Abraham Al-Fāsī the Karaite.* Yale Oriental Series Researches 20–21. New Haven: Yale University Press.

Spanier, Arthur. 1927. *Die Massoretischen Akzente: Eine Darlegung Ihres Systems Nebst Beiträgen zum Verständnis Ihrer Entwicklung.* Veröffentlichungen der Akademie für die Wissenschaft des Judentums. Sprachwissenschaftliche Sektion 1. Bd. Berlin: Akademie-Verlag.

Sperber, Alexander. 1937. "Hebrew based upon Greek and Latin Transliterations." *Hebrew Union College Annual* 12–13: 103–274.

———. 1940. "New Testament and Septuagint." *Journal of Biblical Literature* 59: 193–293.

———. 1966. *A Historical Grammar of Biblical Hebrew. A Presentation of Problems with Suggestions to Their Solution.* Leiden: E.J. Brill.

Steiner, Richard. 1993. "Emphatic פ in the Masoretic Pronunciation of אַפֶּדְנוֹ (Dan 11:45)." In *Hebrew and Arabic Studies in Honour of Joshua Blau*, ed. Haggai Ben-Shammai, 551–561. Tel-Aviv: Tel-Aviv University (in Hebrew).

———. 1996. "Ketiv-ḵerē or polyphony: The שׂ-שׁ distinction according to the Masoretes, the Rabbis, Jerome, Qirqisānī, and Hai Gaon." *Studies in Hebrew and Jewish languages presented to Shelomo Morag*, ed. Moshe Bar-Asher, *151–*179. Jerusalem: Bialik Institute.

———. "משך התנועות בעברית". *Language Studies* 8: 203–227.

Talmon, Raphael. 1998. "A reappraisal of the 'List of ancient Hebrew terms' and the affiliation between Hebrew and Arabic." In *'Ever and 'Arav: Contacts between Arabic Literature and Jewish Literature in the Middle Ages and Modern Times*, ed. Yosef Tobi, 27–51. Tel-Aviv: Tel-Aviv University (in Hebrew).

Talmon, Shemaryahu. 1962. "The three scrolls of the law that were found in the Temple court." *Textus* 2: 14–27.

———. 1970. "The Old Testament text." In *The Cambridge History of the Bible*, ed. Peter R. Ackroyd and Christopher. F Evans, 159–199. Cambridge: Cambridge University Press.

Tov, Emanuel. 1984. "Did the Septuagint translators always understand their Hebrew text?" In *De Septuaginta: Studies in Honour of John William Wevers on His Sixty-Fifth Birthday*, ed. Albert Pietersma and Claude E Cox, 53–70. Mississauga, Ont.: Benben Publications.

———. 1992. *Textual Criticism of the Hebrew Bible*. Minneapolis, Minn: Fortress Press.

———. 1997a. "The scribes of the texts found in the Judean desert." In *The Quest for Context and Meaning: Studies in Biblical Intertextuality in Honor of James A. Sanders*, ed. Craig A Evans and Shemaryahu Talmon, 131–152. Biblical interpretation series v.28. Leiden: Brill.

———. 1997b. *The Text-Critical Use of the Septuagint in Biblical Research*. 2nd ed. Jerusalem biblical studies 8. Jerusalem: Simor.

Tsereteli, Konstantin. 1990. "The Velar Spirant ġ in Modern East Aramaic Dialects." In *Studies in Neo-Aramaic*, ed. Wolfhart Heinrichs, 35–41. Harvard Semitic Studies. Atlanta: Scholars Press.

Versteegh, Cornelis H. M. 1993. *Arabic Grammar and Qurʾānic Exegesis in Early Islam*. Studies in Semitic languages and linguistics 19. Leiden: Brill.

Wutz, Franz. 1925a. "Ist der hebräische Urtext wieder erreichbar?" *Zeitschrift für Alttestamentliche Wissenschaft* 2 N.F. 115–119.

———. 1925b. *Die Transkriptionen von der Septuaginta bis zu Hieronymus.* Beiträge zur Wissenschaft vom Alten Testament n.f., hft. 9. Stuttgart.

Yahalom, Joseph. 1997. *Palestinian Vocalised Piyyuṭ Manuscripts in the Cambridge Genizah Collections.* Cambridge University Library Genizah series 7. Cambridge: Cambridge University Press.

Yeivin, Israel. 1968. *Aleppo Codex.* Jerusalem: Magnes Press, Hebrew University (in Hebrew).

———. 1972. "The forms יקטולנו and יקוטלנו in the scrolls of the Judaean desert in the light of the tradition of Babylonian pointing." In *The Bible and the History of the Jews. Studies in the Bible and in the Literature of the Second Temple Period in Honour of Jacob Lever,* ed. Benjamin Oppenheimer, 258–261. Tel-Aviv: Tel-Aviv University (in Hebrew).

———. 1980. *Introduction to the Tiberian Masorah.* Trans. E. J. Revell. Masoretic studies no. 5. Missoula: Scholars Press.

———. 1981. "From the teachings of the Masoretes." *Textus* 9: 1–27 (in Hebrew).

———. 1985. *The Hebrew Language Tradition as Reflected in the Babylonian Vocalization.* Jerusalem: The Academy of the Hebrew Language (in Hebrew).

———. 2003. *The Biblical Masorah.* Jerusalem: Academy of the Hebrew Language (in Hebrew).

INDEXES

GENERAL INDEX

INDEX OF BIBLICAL REFERENCES

Plate 1   Aleppo codex, fol. 2 recto (Deut. 28:66–29:19)

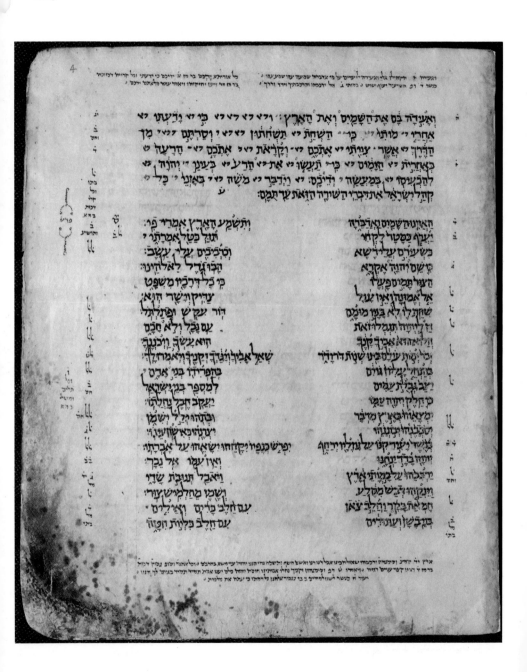

Plate 2   Aleppo codex, fol. 4 recto (Deut. 31:28–32:14)

Plate 3   Aleppo codex, fol. 23 verso (Jud. 4:10–5:10)

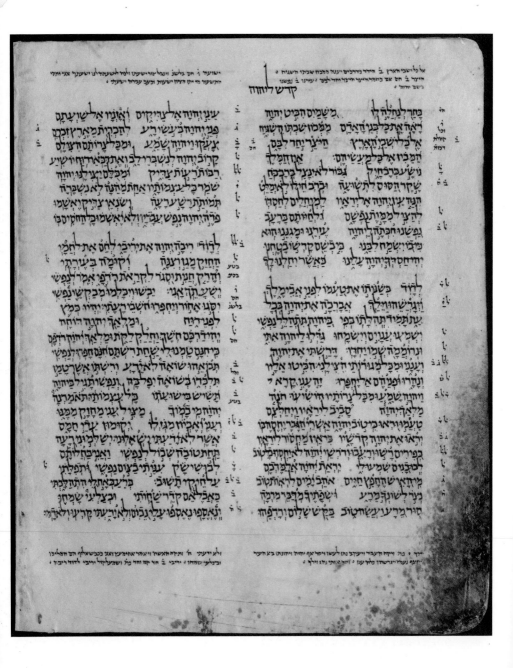

Plate 4   Aleppo codex, fol. 245 verso (Ps. 33:12–35:15)